Made Righteous by Faith

*But let judgment run down as waters,
And righteousness as a mighty stream.*
                              -Amos 5:24

Pastor Mark Spitsbergen, ThD, MS

Made Righteous by Faith
By Dr. Mark Spitsbergen, ThD, MS
Copyright © 2026 by Abiding Place Ministries, San Diego, CA.

ISBN: 979-8-9944098-4-8

Address correspondence to:
Mark Spitsbergen
Abiding Place Ministries
2155 N Campo Truck Trail, Campo CA 91906
www.AbidingPlace.org
AwakeSD@me.com

All rights reserved.

Table of Contents

Introduction 7

Dwell in Me 15

Made. Righteous by The New Birth 20

The Righteous Live by Faith 25

What is Righteousness 31

The Faith of Abraham 39

The Faith of Jesus Christ 46

Grace Through Righteousness Reigns 52

Faith Works, not Law Works 63

Made the Righteousness of God in Him 70

Made the Righteousness of God in Him by the Faith of Jesus Christ 76

Can Faith Alone Make Righteous? 83

Everlasting Righteousness 89

The Fruits of Righteousness 98

Faith and Obedience 105

Law Righteousness 111

Those Who Were Righteous in the Old Testament............121

The Righteousness of Faith Speaks 127

Pleasing in His Sight...134

Conclusion...140

References...143

Glossary of Scriptures..148

Appendix..151

Introduction

"And being found in Him, not having my own righteousness from the Law, but that which is through the faith of Christ: righteousness by the faith from God."

(Php. 3:9)

The first man Adam was born under the reign and rule of God. He was created out of the goodness and love of the Heavenly Father. God placed the man in a Heaven on Earth and everything there was an expression of God's goodness. It would be the place where the man and his family would grow and develop in relationship with God. The one created in the image and likeness of God was given rule over all that God had made upon the Earth. His rule and authority would extend to all who would come forth out of his own life. He was given charge over all the works of God's hands and given the responsibility for the care and well-being of everything there. Although everything that God had given Adam was good, he still disobeyed and did what God had forbidden. When he disobeyed God, he died spiritually and handed over the rulership of his life to sin and death. At that moment,

Adam entered into another world altogether. Adam and all of His descendants entered into a world ruled by the prince and the power of the air, the God of this world, the spirit that works in the children of disobedience[1].

God in His love and mercy would not leave all humanity as the eternal prisoners of sin and death. He would provide a way back into the family once again. God would provide a way for us to enter back into His Kingdom and live in a world ruled by His love and grace[2]. He promised that a Seed of the woman would come, the One Who would destroy the power of sin and death. When the Seed, Christ Jesus, came, He showed us the manner of life that God intended for all humanity to live. Jesus walked out the life of perfect obedience to the Father and demonstrated the ultimate expression of the love of God. As the sinless Lamb of God, He offered up His life for the redemption of all humanity. Through God's great plan of redemption, the life of Jesus would become our life too. His righteousness would be our righteousness – His obedience would become our obedience. Through Him, God not only destroyed the power of sin and death, but also provided the means to forgive any transgressions that might be committed afterward.

Grace through righteousness now reigns by Jesus Christ. Sin reigned over our lives because of Adam's

---
[1] (Eph. 2:2; Rom. 5:12-21)
[2] (Col. 1:13)

transgression, but now through the obedience of Christ Jesus, grace now reigns. God has extended to everyone the fulness of the life and righteousness of His Son[3]. Through the disobedience of Adam, we all died, but now much more through the obedience of Christ Jesus, we are made alive. Through the disobedience of Adam, we were condemned to an eternity of sin and death, but now through the obedience of Christ Jesus, we are no longer under that condemnation. Through the disobedience of Adam, we were made sinners, but now much more through the obedience of Christ Jesus, we are made righteous. As many as will receive Christ Jesus are freed from sin and death and are given the gift of righteousness[4]. Sin and death have lost their power to reign over those in Christ Jesus. Now Adam's death sentence is no longer upon us. The Son has set us free by His obedience and has made His righteousness our own. Because of Adam's sin, we were made sinners and lived in that sin, but now through the righteousness of Jesus, we are made righteous to live in His righteousness[5].

When we were born again, God's own life came into us, and He now lives in us and walks in us[6]. The righteousness that we now have in Him is His life imparted. It's more than the righteousness that Abraham had, because we've

---

[3] (Jn. 1:16; Col. 2:10; Rom. 8:29)
[4] (1 Cor. 1:30; 6:11; Eph. 4:24)
[5] (Rom. 5:19)
[6] (2 Cor. 6:16; Lev. 26:12; Jer. 31:33)

been born again. This righteousness is given to us as a free gift. Along with the gift came the ability to learn how to live out our lives in His righteousness, for we are now all taught of God[7]. His righteousness goes far beyond the righteousness of the Law. This is the righteousness of Christ Jesus Who dwells in us. When Christ Jesus came into our lives, so did His righteousness. The righteousness of Christ Jesus now flows from the sweet fountain of His presence in our lives.

The great proclamation of the Gospel is, "Behold, God has made all things new!" Through the redeeming work of God's Only Begotten Son, old things passed away, and everything became new. God so loved us that He reached down into the pit of debauchery, lifted us out of our iniquity, and clothed us in His righteousness. He gave us His Holy Spirit, the Spirit of Holiness, so that we might live in Him, walk with Him, be led by Him, and taught by Him. By His Spirit, our eyes were open to see what the eyes of men could not see, to hear what the ears could not hear, and to understand those things that could only be taught by the Holy Spirit. We have been recreated in His image and likeness, in righteousness and true holiness. We have been given an abundant life in Christ Jesus. We have been given everything that pertains to life and godliness. We have been given the authority to live as the children of God. We are His temple, the temple of the Holy Spirit.

---

[7] (Jn. 14:17; 16:13-15; 1 Thess. 4:9; 1 Jn. 2:27)

Now the life and righteousness of God is in us like a wellspring and flows out like rivers – all we must do is be willing to live in Him.

In this booklet, we will define righteousness in the context of both the Old and New Testament. The Old Testament saints had a righteousness credited by faith in the coming Redeemer. Today, we have been made the righteousness of God because we have been born again. We will take you through the life of many of the Old Testament saints, which allows us to understand how faith worked in their lives. We will see that there was always a remnant who had faith in the coming Redeemer. It is our hope that you will be able to see the greater glory and righteousness brought to us by the faith of Jesus Christ. The most important point is that God made Jesus our righteousness, and through Him we were born again and received the indwelling righteousness of God. We dwell in Christ Jesus, and His righteousness is our righteousness. He dwells in us, and His righteousness is like a wellspring within. The power of God's own life is at work in us – both the righteousness of God and His holiness. By the work of the Holy Spirit, we learn to do all those things that are pleasing in His sight. Doing those things that are pleasing in the sight of God are not works of self-righteousness. Rather, it's the righteousness that is by the faith of Jesus Christ at work in us.

Made Righteous by Faith

When God found Adam and Eve hiding in their sin and shame, He made a promise of the coming Seed, the Redeemer. The coming Seed is the focus of the entire Old Testament. Abraham believed in the coming Seed and it was credited to him for righteousness[8]. Everyone who believed God's Word was counted righteous, for the righteous "live by faith"[9]. It was faith in the coming Redeemer that reached out and took hold of the provision of redemption before the Redeemer arrived. Every sacrifice of the Old Testament, both before and after the Law, which was given at Mount Sinai, represented the coming Seed. Some understood it and saw His day, and others were just lost in a religious ritual that they thought was the way to be righteous. Yet, everywhere that we observe faith in the Old Testament is about the coming Seed.

Abraham received an imputed righteousness, but through the New Birth something far greater has taken place in us. We not only have righteousness accounted to us, we are actually in the true righteous One, Christ Jesus. Abraham was not presented before the Father in Christ Jesus, but we are, we have been born again! Abraham was given a promise of the coming Seed and believing what God said, he had righteousness credited to him.

---

[8] (Gen. 15:4-6; 21:12; Gal. 3:16, 19)
[9] (Hab. 2:4)

Now Christ Jesus, having been exalted to the right hand of God, presents us in Himself before the Father. We are in Christ Jesus, presented before God in Him. Abraham did not have this kind of righteousness. This is far more than just imputed righteousness; this is righteousness that comes by being in Christ Jesus. When we were born again, we were born into the family of God and washed with the water of regeneration, and renewed in the Holy Spirit. We have what no one else before Christ Jesus had, a new heart and a new spirit. Now being made righteous, we are presented before the Presence of God in the righteousness and holiness of Jesus Christ. All that we are before the Father, and all that we have in our lives, is from Jesus. God has made Him to be our wisdom, righteousness, holiness and redemption. We dwell in Christ and our lives are hidden in Him. He presents us before the Father on the basis of who He is. We are honored, however, to have Him revealed through our lives by the Holy Spirit. From the very moment that we are born again we have His righteousness and can never be any more righteous.

Now having been made righteous, God the Holy Spirit works in us, to mature us, in all that has been fully granted to us, in Christ Jesus. Christ Jesus is in us by the Holy Spirit which He has given to us. It is God who now works in us and through us. He establishes us and matures us in all that the Father has[10]. The Holy Spirit is the power source of the righteousness of God in us. By the Holy Spirit, we mature in the outworking of all the ways of God in our lives, while all the time we are presented in Christ Jesus: holy and without blemish and blameless[11]. God has called us to a holy communion in which we are to dwell in Christ Jesus and He dwells in us[12].

---

[10] (John 16:14)
[11] (Col 1:22)
[12] (John 6:56)

Dwell in Me

"He that eats my flesh, and drinks my blood, dwells in me, and I in him."

-(Jn 6:56)

Jesus said, come and dwell in Me[13]. God has done a wonderful thing for us through Christ Jesus: He has invited us to dwell in Him. We not only dwell in Him, but He dwells in us. As we dwell in Christ Jesus He presents us to the Father with His righteousness and His holiness. In fact, the whole of our lives and existence is found in Him[14]. His life was not only imputed unto us but was also imparted when we were born again. Now His righteousness and Holiness dwells in us and flows out of us as we yield to Him. Just as Christ Jesus dwelled in the Father and the Father dwelled in Him, He now dwells in us and we dwell in Him[15]. He likens this mutual indwelling to a branch dwelling in a vine. As the branch draws its life from the vine even so we draw our life from Christ Jesus. We cannot do anything without Him but if

---

[13] (Jn. 15:4)
[14] (Gal. 2:20; Col. 2:13; 3:13; Eph. 2:6; 1 Cor. 6:19-20)
[15] (Jn. 14:20, 23; 17:22-23)

we continue to dwell in Him we bring forth the fruits of His life[16]. He made this mutual indwelling possible through the sacrifice of Himself for our sins. Through the giving of His own life on the cross He destroyed the power of sin and death and cleansed us with His own blood. He purified us from all iniquity and gave us a new life in Himself[17]. The invitation now exists for all to come and dwell in Him[18]. He offered up His life to make this possible. He gave His body and His blood so that we might live by Him. As the bread of life His body became our spiritual food. His blood was given to us as a spiritual drink that His life might dwell in us. The communion that each person may have results in a mutual indwelling with Jesus[19]. The very moment that we are born again, we are given His life, His righteousness, His holiness, and His relationship with the Father. The life of Jesus becomes our life and we find ourselves complete in Him[20]. Just as Jesus lived His life in the Father and the Father dwelled in Him, He dwells in us and we are to live our lives in Him[21]. Our bodies are made His holy dwelling place and the members of Christ[22]. He has held nothing back from us of His life

---

[16] (Jn. 15:1-8)
[17] (Tt. 2:14)
[18] (Jn. 15:4)
[19] (Jn. 5:56; 14:20, 23, 15:1-7; 17:21-23; 1 Jn. 3:34; 4:15-16; Eph. 5:30; 1 Cor. 12:27; etc)
[20] (Col. 2:11-12)
[21] (Jn. 14:17-23; 17:23)
[22] (1 Jn. 3:24; 1 Cor. 3:16; 12:27)

and called us to be conformed to His image[23]. He has given us all of His fullness and now by dwelling in His love we mature and are filled with all the fullness of God[24]. As we live our lives in Him we grow up into Him in all things[25].

Once again we do not have to present ourselves before God on the basis of who we are. Rather, we are presented before God in Christ Jesus[26]. We do not come to the Father to be accepted on the basis of what we have done but what Christ Jesus has done for us. Our response to all that He has done is to present our bodies holy and acceptable to God as His dwelling place[27]. We are to yield our members to Him as the servants of righteousness[28]. We are to live and dwell in the Holy Spirit who leads us and guides us into all the ways of God. Our lives are now hidden away in Christ Jesus and for us to live is Christ. As God hid Moses away in the cleft of the rock even so He hides our lives away in Jesus. Jesus said that the work which He did was by the Father and now we have the same union. The work that we do is by the work of Christ Jesus who works in us[29]. Christ Jesus is the power source for all God's righteousness and His holiness that works

---

[23] (Rom. 8:29; 2 Cor. 3:18; Col 3:10)
[24] (Jn. 1:16; Eph. 3:20)
[25] (Eph. 4:15)
[26] (Col 1:22, 28; 1 Cor 1:30; 6:11)
[27] (Rom 12:1)
[28] (Rom 6:16-22)
[29] (Jn. 10:38; 15:5; Php. 1:11; Col. 1:29; 1 Cor. 15:10; Heb. 13:21; etc)

within our lives. We yield ourselves to Him as those alive from the dead. We yield ourselves as servants of righteousness and He brings everything about our lives into perfect conformity to the will of the Father[30]. We bring every thought into captivity to the obedience of Christ by the power of God[31]. We keep ourselves in the keeping work of Christ Jesus[32]. We can now boldly say that as He is, so are we in this world[33]. We are able to walk even as He walks[34]. We are able to overcome just as He overcame because He dwells in us[35]. Jesus is the fountainhead and well spring of the life of God and the rivers of the Holy Spirit which issue forth from our lives. Our bodies are the dwelling place of God and so they are called the temples of the Holy Spirit[36]. All we must do is imitate Christ and follow His leadership[37].

Christ Jesus is our life and for us to live is Christ. We dwell in Him and are hidden away in Him. When Christ Jesus who is our life appears we also appear with Him in glory, we are both in Him and with Him[38]. Still, it must not be forgotten that each one of us individually will give an account for the deeds done in our bodies[39]. He is our

---

[30] (Rom. 6:19-22)
[31] (2 Cor. 10:4-5)
[32] (1 Jn. 5:18; 1 Pet. 1:5)
[33] (1 Jn. 4:12)
[34] (1 John 2:6)
[35] (1 Jn. 4:4; Rev. 3:21)
[36] (1 Cor. 3:16; 2 Cor. 6:16-17)
[37] (Eph. 5:1; Mt. 16:24)
[38] (Col. 3:1-3)
[39] (2 Cor. 5:10; Rom. 14:10)

life and our glory and without Him we can do nothing. Yet by Him we can do all things through Christ Jesus who strengthens us. In this glorious life of the Spirit we can now live and dwell in God's love and by dwelling in His love we have the witness that we dwell in God and God dwells in us[40]. As we yield ourselves to Him, His life flows out of us like rivers of living water.

---

[40] (1 Jn. 4:15-16; Col. 1:27; 1 Jn. 3:24)

Made. Righteous by The New Birth

"He saved us, not by works of righteousness that we have done, but according to His mercy, by the washing of regeneration and renewing of the Holy Spirit."

(Tt. 3:5)

The Apostle Paul perfectly defines salvation when He says,

*"but when the goodness and loving kindness of God our Savior appeared, **He saved us**, not by works of righteousness that we have done, but according to His mercy, by the **washing of regeneration and renewing of the Holy Spirit**, which He poured out richly through Jesus Christ our Savior. So that being made **righteous by His grace** we should be heirs according to the expectation of eternal life."*

(Tt. 3:4–7)

Every definition of what it means to be saved by grace must include being born again. Regeneration is another way of saying that we have been born again. The price was paid by the blood of Jesus so that all men might be washed with the water of regeneration. The theme of the New Testament and of Jesus' ministry is introduced when He said "you must be born again." Through the new birth we were made everything that is acceptable to God. There is nothing that describes the new creation more perfectly than,

> "old things passed away and behold **all things** are new."
>
> (2 Cor. 5:17)

By grace we were saved! The work of grace describes us as the workmanship of God created in Christ Jesus[41]. In this new creation, God's righteousness is revealed.

Righteousness could not come by the Law. The Law was not given to make someone righteous. The Law was given to make sin appear exceedingly sinful. The Law was given by God and it was spiritual but was powerless to change the heart of man. The Law could not impart the life of God, but instead could only reveal sin. God's plan was to bring forth a Seed, not a Law. It was His plan to redeem man and bring them back into oneness with Himself. It was God's desire to bring forth a new creation.

---

[41] (Eph. 2:8-9)

It was God's desire to break the stronghold of sin and iniquity that imprisoned the lives of men. His purpose was to set us free from all the claims of death and sin that possessed men because of disobedience.

The Law was the means by which God consecrated a family to bring forth His Son. To raise His Son under the Law and the commandments of the Lord[42]. All those under the Law were as those under tutors and governors to bring them to something far better than the Law. The Law was only a shadow of good things to come and not the very image[43]. The Law could never bring forth the promise of God because it was weak depending upon human ability[44]. The Law was no more the provision and remedy for the spiritual condition of men than Ismael was the promised son of Abraham[45]. The Law could only point to the Redeemer and Life-giver but could never redeem and impart the life of God to sinful man[46].

God promised to bring forth a New Covenant through which He could create within His people a new heart and a new spirit and put His Spirit within us[47]. It was for this purpose that God came, and lived, and died and rose again to establish a New Covenant. The Word was made flesh so that we could be born of the word and have the

---

[42] (Gal. 4:4)
[43] (Heb. 10:1)
[44] (Rom. 8:3)
[45] (Gal. 4:21-31)
[46] (Gal. 3:21)
[47] (Ezek. 26:36)

laws and commandments of the Lord written on our hearts and minds[48]. This is the faith that Jesus announced to Nicodemus the ruler of the Jews. Mankind would need to be born again! They were born in sin under the dominion of sin, but now God had provided a way for them to be born of God by the Spirit of God to live under the reign of God, and the ministry of righteousness[49]. All of the Old Testament prophecies concerning the New Covenant described a change that would take place in the heart of man. The New Covenant would empower His people to walk in His ways and keep His judgments and commandments[50].

The New Covenant is God's redemption fulfilled. It's the fulfillment of the promise made in the garden to restore our fellowship with Him. It's the covenant that the Lord finds no fault in because through it He gave us everything that we need to live the life He created man to have[51]. We are made into everything that is holy and acceptable to God in Christ Jesus[52]. God gave us all His fullness and made us complete in His Son. God's salvation matures and establishes us in all His ways all we have to do is follow[53]. Through His great salvation we received His

---

[48] (Heb. 8:10; 10:16)
[49] (2 Cor 3:9)
[50] (Jer. 31:31-34; Ezek. 36:25-37; Heb. 8:10; 10:16)
[51] (Heb. 8:7-8)
[52] (Rom 12:1; 1 Thess. 5:24; 1 Cor. 1:30; 6:11)
[53] (Eph 4:13, 15; 2 Pet. 3:18)

own righteousness as a gift, and as those made righteous we live by His faith[54].

The life of God came into our lives through Christ Jesus. His life came in – not in part, but in full[55]. He came with His righteousness, holiness, and goodness – all that He is. His life became our life, so that we may say, "for me to live is Christ." His life became the source of our life like a branch in the vine[56]. His righteousness and Holiness became our righteousness and holiness. God gave us His wisdom and righteousness and holiness when we were born again[57]. This is more than many are willing to believe, but still, God gave all of this to us in Christ Jesus. We are now complete in Him. As the workmanship of God created in Christ Jesus, we now have the ability to live out our lives in Him by the Holy Spirit. We have His grace and mercy so that we might grow up into all that He has given us.

---

[54] (Gal. 2:20; Php. 3:9)
[55] (Jn. 1:16; Eph. 3:19; Col. 1:27)
[56] (Jn. 15:1-7)
[57] (1 Cor. 1:30; Jer. 23:5-6; 2 Cor. 5:21; Eph. 4:24)

The Righteous Live by Faith

"Behold, his soul which is lifted up is not upright in him, but the righteous shall live by his faith."

(Hab. 2:4)

The prophet Habakkuk was the first person to say that the "righteous live by faith" (וְצַדִּיק בֶּאֱמוּנָתוֹ יִחְיֶה, 've-saddiq be-emunato yichyeh') (Hab. 2:4). He contrasts the righteous who live by faith to those who refuse to hear the word of the Lord, by saying, "the soul who is lifted up is not upright." The Hebrew word ישר ('yashar', "upright") has a close relationship to צַדִּיק ('saddiq', "righteous"). The upright who believe the word of the Lord are the ones shown to be righteous. Refusal to believe God is the pride and arrogance of self will. Those who are not upright and righteous refuse to cooperate with what God has spoken. These are the ones who refuse to believe the word of God. It was a terrible thing in the ears of the people to hear the prophet Habakuk say that they would go into captivity. It

Made Righteous by Faith

was contrary to everything they believed about themselves and God.

The Apostle Paul repeats the same words spoken by the prophet Habakkuk in the context of the New Testament faith. Just as those that Habakkuk spoke to refused to believe the word of the Lord, there were the same kind of people in Paul's day. When the message, "You must be born again," came, they rejected it. They refused to hear that righteousness by the Law had come to an end. They would rather walk after their own concepts of God's will and continue to seek to be made righteous by the Law than to agree with God's word. Just as in the days of Habakkuk the people refused to hear the words of God that Paul was preaching. Their refusal changed nothing- the righteousness of God was revealed from heaven to anyone who would hear and believe. Their rejection of the invitation was their rejection of faith and righteousness by faith. Jesus announced the new and living way, the New Covenant. He made it very clear: no one can be right with God through the Law[58]. To the religious Jews this announcement would have been more infuriating than what Habakkuk said to the religious Jews of his day. Still, **the only way to be right with God was to hear the word of the Lord and believe.**

There were many who responded to the word of the Lord in the Old Testament and, like Abraham, believed

---

[58] (Gal. 3:11)

God and it was accounted to them for righteousness. Like Abraham, they walked with God by faith. Enoch walked with God and so pleased God that He was translated into heaven. There were others in the Old Testament that pleased God, and we know that they walked by faith because without faith it's impossible to please God[59]. Abraham, Isaac and Jacob walked with God. Moses, Joshua and Samuel walked with God, and many more that are named in the Old Testament. When Paul spoke of the great exploits of faith and of the great cloud of witnesses from the Old Testament, he named those who believed what God had spoken, and therefore were the righteous who live by faith[60]. They all had one thing in common: they all believed God and being moved by faith obeyed. Each of the many examples of those who heard the word of the Lord and believed had a corresponding action of obedience[61].

The righteous live by faith because they believe God's report and it's counted unto them for righteousness. Before Christ Jesus purchased our salvation, there were many who put their faith in the coming Redeemer. Job is one of the great examples of a man who walked with God. Job was perfect and upright who said,

---

[59] (Heb. 11:5-6)
[60] (Heb. 10:38)
[61] (Heb. 11:4-38)

"I know my Redeemer lives and will stand on the Earth on the last day."

(Job 19:25)

Abraham was the friend of God, who believed God's report of the coming Seed and was credited with righteousness. Moses was allowed to see God in the fullness of His glory and had the revelation of the Prophet Who God would raise up, Christ Jesus[62]. David was a man after God's own heart who sang the prophecies of the coming Redeemer. Isaiah was the one whose sin was taken away and his iniquity purged when He saw redemption complete[63]. God put His word in Jeremiah's mouth and told of the days of the New Covenant[64]. Daniel was a man greatly beloved of God to whom God showed that the Messiah would be cut off for the sins of the people[65]. Simeon was a righteous man to whom it was revealed that he would see the Messiah before he died[66]. Zachariah and Elizabeth were both righteous before the Lord and gave birth to the one who would prepare the way of the Lord[67]. Mary was highly favored by God and Joseph was a righteous man[68]. All of the prophets of old were referred to as holy men through whom the Holy Spirit spoke. All of

---

[62] (Deut. 18:15; Ac. 3:22; 7:37)
[63] (Isa. 6:1-12)
[64] (Jer. 31:34; Heb. 10:16; 2 Cor. 6:16)
[65] (Dan. 9:6)
[66] (Lk. 2:25-26)
[67] (Lk. 1:5-6)
[68] (Mt. 1:19)

them prophesied of the One Who was to come and the glory that would follow[69].

Today, the righteousness which is by faith comes simply by calling on the name of Jesus and being born again. Righteousness is not just created to us it is imparted for redemption has come and we live in the days of the reign of Christ Jesus. The Promised Seed has come and was born 2,000 years ago in Bethlehem. If we will believe the promise just as Abraham did, we will receive the promise. All of the Old Testament saints looked forward to the day and put their faith in His coming. We look back to the day that He came and we are made righteous. Once again, today it's not just a righteousness credited to us but one that is imparted because we, unlike those before Christ Jesus, have been born again.

The call of God is for all men to repent and turn from sin and be empowered to live by His Spirit. We are called to surrender our lives to God who washes us in the blood of His Son Jesus and recreates us in Him by the Holy Spirit. Through one simple act of turning to Jesus Christ, God sets us free from the law of sin and death (Rom. 8:2). He transforms our nature and life[70]. He makes us righteous in Christ, giving us the righteousness of His Only Begotten Son Christ Jesus[71]. By the testimony of His

---

[69] (1 Pet. 1:11-12)
[70] (2 Cor. 5:17–18; 1 Cor. 6:11; Tt. 3:5)
[71] (1 Cor. 1:30; 2 Cor. 5:21; Rom. 4:1–25; 10:6–13)

own life, He condemned sin in the flesh so that the righteousness of the Law might be fulfilled in us[72].

---

[72] (Rom. 8:3)

What is Righteousness

"The LORD is righteous in all His ways, and holy in all His works."

(Ps. 145:17)

Righteousness can only be defined by God. He is the only true measure of that which is right. Men know very little about righteousness, and if we define it in the context of our lives we would be wrong. God defines righteousness in the context of His ways. God alone is the judge of whether or not an action or deed is right. Those actions which He judges to be right are acts of righteousness. The world of sin and iniquity is a world of unrighteousness, and men have been imprisoned in it. The many scriptures on righteousness help us to clearly categorize what righteousness is. It's everything that is not sin and iniquity! The word righteous was first used in contrast to the iniquity of the world that was beyond all possibility of redemption[73]. God called Noah a צַדִּיק ('saddiq') righteous. The person who is a 'saddiq' is a person who is righteous before God in contrast to the

---
[73] (Gen. 6:9; 7:1)

wicked world around him. The Hebrew word is translated as "righteous" or "just" and is found 206 times in the Hebrew Bible (BHS). The Hebrew word 'saddiq' is translated by the Septuagint using the Greek word δίκαιος ('dikaios'). These words, whether Hebrew or Greek are used in contrast to wickedness[74]. When all of the words belonging to the root צדק ('sadaq') are considered, there is a lot of context to define this word properly. When we consider every usage of the root, it occurs 523 times in the Old Testament[75]. The word, whether in Hebrew or Greek, means "being right," specifically being righteous or upright with God. It was the righteous who were important to both God and Abraham when the destruction of Sodom and Gomorrah was being considered[76]. The days of Noah and also of Sodom and Gomorrah are the context for the first two occurrences of צַדִּיק ('saddiq'), in both instances it is used in contrast to those who do iniquity.

The New Testament definition of righteousness is the same as its Hebrew counterpart and is derived from the Greek root δικη ('dike'), which means "justice"[77]. We might say that at the very heart of righteousness is God's justice and truth.

---

[74] (Gen. 7:1)
[75] (see Appendix 1)
[76] (Gen. 18:23-26, 28)
[77] (see Appendix 1)

"The richness of the Heb. usage is in general excellently reproduced in the corresponding LXX words δίκη, δικαιοσύνη, δίκαιος, and δικαιοῦν."

(Gottlob Schrenk, 1964)

In both the Old Testament and in the New Testament, God's righteousness extends into His redemptive goodness in which He offers to all mankind the opportunity to be redeemed. He shows Himself to be righteous in providing the means for mankind to become righteous. All of our righteousness is found in Christ Jesus. We have the righteousness of Christ Jesus because we are in Him. We also have His righteousness flowing through us because Christ Jesus is in us. This mutual indwelling provides us with the righteousness of God at the time that we are born again. We stand before God in the righteousness of Jesus and Jesus stands within us bringing into our lives the fruits of His righteousness.

Taking into account that "righteous" and "righteousness" are found about 144 times in the New Testament, it would take considerable space to deal with every context- but in general we know that God is righteous and He requires righteousness from His people. The parents of John the Baptizer were righteous because they walked in all the commandments and ordinances of God blamelessly[78]. The declaration through Zachariah,

---

[78] (Lk. 1:6)

Made Righteous by Faith

John's father, was that redemption through the Messiah would result in His people being able to serve Him in holiness and righteousness[79]. God's people are supposed to seek/desire His righteousness just as they seek/desire His Kingdom[80]. We are to hunger and thirst for righteousness[81]. The righteous are set in contrast to the wicked on the day of judgement because of their righteous deeds[82]. In summary, there is a righteousness that God expects for us to live in. It's the righteousness of a living faith. The righteousness of God that we have because of the active working of Christ Jesus in our lives. Christ Jesus who lives and dwells in us brings forth His righteousness through our lives. The righteousness of God is the living activity of Christ Jesus in our lives. Righteousness is based upon believing God's word, but is manifested in our lives by the operation of God through our lives.

Righteousness is not a mere mental assent- it is evidenced by a transformed life, where actions and conduct reflect the inner work of grace. Righteousness is a word that describes the conduct of a person in the eyes of God. It is always used in association to men obeying God and walking in the moral laws of God. What should be obvious to all is that righteousness is the opposite of unrighteousness. The unrighteous are those who refuse

---

[79] (Lk. 1:75)
[80] (Mt. 6:33)
[81] (Mt. 5:6)
[82] (Mt. 25:37)

the ways of God. God has judged the world on the basis of men's response to His moral laws and will again judge the world in righteousness. God judged the world in the days of Noah for their unrighteousness. Adam's children became so wicked in about 1,656 years that God had to destroy them because of their unrighteousness. Still, even after that the judgments of God were perfectly known the descendants of Noah soon returned to their unrighteousness. The unrighteousness bound in the heart of men only has one cure. Without the new birth, men are the children of disobedience ruled by the god of this world, Satan[83]. Jesus said that He would judge all mankind in the future and that judgment would be based on the word which He spoke[84].

God's record of man has given witness to very few men that were righteous. In the first age of men (that lasted about 1,656 years), God called Abel, the son of Adam, "righteous;"[85] and Enoch, who was seven generations removed from Adam, and although he was not specifically called "righteous," he pleased God[86]. Finally Noah, who was the great grandson of Enoch, was called "righteous" by God[87]. What made these men righteous in the midst of such an ungodly and wicked world? Abel was described to

---

[83] (Eph 2:2; Gal 1:4)
[84] (Jn 12:48; Acts 17:31)
[85] (Mt. 23:35)
[86] (Mt. 23:35; 1 Jn. 3:10; Heb. 11:4)
[87] (Gen. 7:1)

be righteous because of his worship of God and His faith in the coming Redeemer. Enoch was a man who walked with God and he pleased God. All we really know about Him was that He preached against ungodliness and warned men of the coming judgment of God[88]. (Ungodliness can be considered as a synonym of unrighteous). The few things that we know about Noah were that his relationship with God was such that he could hear the voice of God and that He was a preacher of righteousness who stood in contrast to the ungodly[89]. The ungodly and the unrighteous are both defined in the same way – they are those who walk in sin and iniquity.

The righteousness of God is revealed throughout the Bible. God, Who is holy, is shown to be holy by His righteousness[90].

> "The LORD is righteous in all His ways, and holy in all His works."
>
> (Ps. 145:17)

All of God's actions are bound to His judgments. His judgment of what is right and wrong and what is good and evil. God's ways are summarized in the song of Moses,

> "He is the Rock – His <u>work</u> is perfect, for all His <u>ways</u> are judgment. A God of truth and without iniquity,

---

[88] (Jude 1:14-15)
[89] (2 Pet. 2:5)
[90] (Isa. 5:16)

righteous (צַדִּיק, 'saddiq') *and upright* (יָשָׁר, 'yashar') *is He."*

(Dt. 32:4)

All of God's actions are perfect, because all of His ways are right. He is righteous – the righteous LORD will do no iniquity[91]. Paul also made this contrast between righteousness and iniquity many times. The goodness of God is upon those who live by faith and His wrath is on the unrighteousness[92]. The righteousness of God has been revealed through the New Covenant which established His righteousness in the heart of those who are born again. Whereas the wrath of God is still and more profoundly revealed against all ungodliness and unrighteousness of men, who would hold the truth in unrighteousness[93]. Throughout the history of mankind righteousness has been described on the basis of those who are willing to agree with God. We are to agree with God that Christ Jesus is our righteousness. We are to agree with God that we are to live our lives in Christ Jesus.

Once again, it is only God's righteousness that defines the meaning of righteousness. The ways of God define "the rules" of a faithful and right relationship that men are to have with Him as well as with their fellow man. Righteousness in full is understood by the love of God.

---

[91] (Zeph. 3:5)
[92] (Rom 1:17-18)
[93] (Rom. 1:18)

Righteousness covers every dimension of our walk with God and the order of a proper social relationship, which includes every dimension of our moral conduct. Of course, the highest standard of righteousness is the "righteousness of God." God has supplied us with His own righteousness that comes by the gift of salvation. He has poured His love into our hearts by the Holy Spirit so that His love might be manifested through us. The manifestation of His love through our lives is the manifestation of His righteousness. We have the righteousness of God because He gave us a new heart and a new spirit to receive it, and the power of the Holy Spirit to live it. The righteousness of God is the wellspring and source of all God's righteousness manifested in our lives.

The Faith of Abraham

*"And he brought him forth abroad, and said, 'Look now toward Heaven, and tell the stars, if you are able to number them,' and He said to him, 'So shall **your seed** be.' And he believed in the LORD; and He counted it to him for righteousness."*

(Gen. 15:5–6)

The faith of Abraham is how the Apostle Paul established the doctrine of righteousness by faith in the New Covenant. The faith of Abraham was not only credited to Him for righteousness[94], but was also demonstrated by His actions[95]. Righteousness was credited to Abraham because he believed God's word concerning the coming Seed[96]. There were many things that God told Abraham which Abraham believed and subsequently obeyed. But there is one thing that stands out above all others: he believed God regarding a Seed, a

---

[94] (Rom. 3:22; 4:5)
[95] (Jas. 2:21-24)
[96] (Gen. 15:6)

promised son. What's most important about that promise[97] was highlighted by the Apostle Paul,

> "Now to Abraham and his Seed were the promises made. He said not, 'And to seeds,' as of many; but as of one, 'And to your Seed,' Who is Christ."
>
> (Gal. 3:17)

Receiving righteousness was all about receiving Christ Jesus, Who was the promised Seed.

Abraham obeyed the voice of God and kept the charge of God[98]. He kept God's commandments and statutes and laws before the Law of Moses was given, **but it was in his faith in the coming Seed that he found redemption and righteousness.** Since the transgression of Adam men were under the power of sin and death. There was nothing that anyone could do that would remove that power. There were no works of righteousness that could make them righteous in the eyes of God. The only thing that could make a person righteous was faith in the redeemer, the coming Seed. Only Jesus Christ would be able to remove mens' sin and destroy the power of death that bound all mankind. Righteousness could only be found in Him who through His death delivered us from sin so that we could live in righteousness[99].

---

[97] (Gen. 13:15; 17:8; 22:18)
[98] (Gen. 26:5)
[99] (1 Pet. 2:24)

When Abraham died he was still in need of redemption and was confined to "Abraham's bosom."[100] He died in faith having not received the promise but embraced it[101]. Those under the first covenant had to wait for redemption that could only come through the shed blood of Jesus Christ[102]. Even though Abraham was credited with righteousness still he had to wait until Christ Jesus went down into hell to lead captivity captive and liberate them from the power of death[103]. Abraham was not made or created anew in righteousness, rather he had righteousness credited to him because he believed.

Abraham's righteousness had nothing to do with Law-works but instead had everything to do with his willingness to believe in the coming Redeemer. We learn from James[104] that his righteousness was proven by his obedience, but this does not contradict what Paul revealed. God confirmed the righteousness that was credited to Abraham when Abraham obeyed God and was willing to sacrifice His son, which was also a great witness to God's sacrifice of His only begotten Son. The partnership and friendship that Abraham had with God was witnessed in Abraham's willingness to obey God no matter what was asked of him[105].

---

[100] (Lk. 16:19-31)
[101] (Heb. 11:13)
[102] (Heb. 9:15)
[103] (Eph. 4:8-9; 1 Pet. 3:18-19; Lk. 16:2; 23:43)
[104] (Jas. 2:21-23)
[105] (Gen. 22:1-19)

The promise to Abraham and his seed of being the heir of the world, once again, had everything to do with his willingness to believe in the coming Redeemer and nothing to do with works[106]. If the promise to Abraham were to be made void then faith would also be made void[107]. Once again, faith was and is all about the Redeemer, Christ Jesus – the One Who would destroy the power of Adam's disobedience held over all mankind. Abraham's obedience could not eliminate Adam's disobedience. Abraham was bound by the sin and death of Adam like everyone else, only the coming Seed could break the power of sin and death that held him. There was no amount of obedience that could make him righteous. The only place that faith and deliverance can be found is in Christ Jesus. The only place that righteousness can be found is in Christ Jesus. The only way that a person can be made righteous is by the faith of Christ Jesus.

The faith of Abraham can only be defined by his belief in the coming Seed, the One who makes righteous[108]. The remarkable faith which Abraham had is demonstrated throughout his life, however most important Abraham was shown to be unwavering in his faith in the coming Redeemer, The Seed, and specifically the miracle birth planned by God which every natural indication said could not happen. Sarah was far beyond the natural ability to get

---

[106] (Rom. 4:13)
[107] (Rom. 4:14, 16)
[108] (Rom. 4:16)

pregnant and had been barren for their whole union. Even Abraham himself was beyond the normal years of being able to participate in the coming Seed. However, **he did not stagger at the promise.** Abraham was fully persuaded that the promise of God to him would bring to pass the promise of the coming Redeemer for himself and all mankind[109]. He was fully persuaded that the Redeemer would come through his own body and that of Sarah's. It was because of this that righteousness was credited to him[110].

We would not be regarding the whole counsel of God if we did not recognize the obedience that existed in the relationship that Abraham had with God. In many respects it actually defined his relationship with God. He left his home and went out to a land unknown to him. He left not knowing where he was going[111]. His obedience to God ultimately culminated in his willingness to sacrifice the promised one that would be the means by which the Messiah would come into the world. Every act of obedience expressed by Abraham was an expression of his faith in the coming Seed, the Redeemer. Just as Noah, who became an heir of righteousness by faith because he believed God, a belief that was always accompanied by obedience wherever it was witnessed[112].

---

[109] (Jn. 8:56; Gal. 3:16; Mt. 13:17; Heb. 11:13)
[110] (Rom. 4:22)
[111] (Heb. 11:8)
[112] (Heb. 11:7)

Made Righteous by Faith

One of the most important points that Paul is making is that, just like Abraham, the Gentiles are also credited with righteousness without Law-works. Just like Abraham, anyone who would have faith in the Seed, Christ Jesus, would be saved and thus made righteous. Although Abraham's salvation was one looking to the coming Redeemer, the Gentiles would be able to receive the full blessings of the promise fulfilled. Although Abraham exhibited extraordinary obedience towards God, still he had no "Law works" or "Law obedience" to boast in for righteousness[113].

Righteousness is credited to us in the same way as Abraham, because we believe in Christ Jesus for righteousness and not in Law-works. Even more it is credited because we have believed that God raised Jesus from the dead[114]. The promise does not end with the message of Romans 4, it has gone far beyond just having righteousness credited to us because, by the new birth, we are made the righteousness of God[115]. Many Jews had turned the laws of God into a reward system, but Paul is underscoring that there is no such thing with God. Therefore, any Gentile who simply believes and calls on the name of Jesus for salvation is instantly made righteous at the time of the new birth, without any Law-works. With the same words Paul brings down the need for

---

[113] (Rom. 4:4-5)
[114] (Rom. 4:24)
[115] (Rom. 5:19; 2 Cor. 5:21)

circumcision for righteousness, pointing out that Abraham was credited for righteousness prior to being circumcised[116]. Righteousness by faith is revealed to be not by Law-works, but by the promise of God to redeem man. Paul moves deeper into the righteousness that we have received by taking us to the resurrection of Jesus. It was the life-imparting power through the resurrection of Jesus Christ from the dead that brought righteousness to us[117]. We have received the inward resurrection. Raised up to the eternal life of God that is in Christ Jesus[118]. Jesus is the One "who was delivered for our offences, and was raised again to make us righteous." (Rom. 4:25) There is no other way to be righteous before God!

---

[116] (Rom. 4:9, 12)
[117] (Rom. 1:4; 4:17, 24; 10:9–10; Col. 3:1-3)
[118] (Col. 3:1-3; Eph. 2:6)

The Faith of Jesus Christ

"in Whom we have boldness and access by confidence through His faith."

(Eph 3:12)

There is only one kind of faith, but it is expressed in several different ways. There is the faith of Jesus Christ[119], the faith of the Gospel[120], the faith of God[121] and the faith of Abraham[122]. All of these expressions of faith find their commonality in Jesus. The New Testament is all about the faith of Jesus Christ. There is not a unique faith that belongs to the four Gospels and then a different kind of faith that belongs to the Pauline epistles or any of the other epistles. It is the faith of Jesus Christ that made us righteous. It is the faith of Jesus Christ that delivered us from the Law. It is by the faith of Jesus Christ that we are

---

[119] (Rom. 3:22; Gal. 2:16, 20, 22; Eph. 3:12; Php. 3:9; Jas. 2:1)
[120] (Php. 1:27)
[121] (Rom. 3:3)
[122] (Rom. 4:12, 16)

delivered from sin and death[123]. It is by the faith of Jesus Christ that we were born again[124]. It is by the faith of Jesus Christ that we were saved and washed with the water of regeneration[125].

Righteousness by faith is the righteousness that comes by the faith of Jesus Christ, our faith is the faith that he supplied. Christ Jesus has given to us His faith and the results of His faith, this new life in Him. The faith that was found in those that interacted with Jesus in the four Gospels was always about what each person believed that Jesus was able to do for them. They did not have faith apart from Christ Jesus. When the blind men came to Jesus, He asked them if they believed that He could open their eyes, their reply was, "Yes, Lord," and then they were healed, according to their faith. Their faith was what they believed Jesus could do for them[126]. So it is with us today – it's not our faith that makes us righteous, but what we know that Jesus has done for us[127]. He made us righteous when we were born again and He came into our lives[128]. The righteousness that we now have in Christ Jesus is defined is not our own but His righteousness. We cannot think of ourselves as righteous apart from the new

---

[123] (Rom. 8:3)
[124] (Jn. 3:3-6)
[125] (Tt. 3:5)
[126] (Mt. 9:27-29)
[127] (1 Cor. 1:30; 6:11)
[128] (1 Jn. 3:24; 4:4; Col. 1:27; Php. 3:9)

birth and the indwelling of Christ Jesus[129]. When we were born again, we were given all things that pertain to life and godliness[130]. We were given God's righteousness and holiness[131]. We were given a new heart and a new spirit. We were empowered to live the life of God!

We are able to witness the magnitude of Jesus' faith throughout the pages of the four Gospels. He raised the dead, walked on the water, and fed the multitudes with a few loaves and fishes. Jesus went to the cross by His faith; He went down into Hell by His faith; He was raised from the dead by His faith[132]. Now, every person that has been born again is made the righteousness of God by His faith. It is Jesus' faith that is the faith of the Gospel. We can also say that the faith of Jesus is the faith of God. The righteousness of God that was brought to us by Jesus Christ is the Righteousness that was witnessed by the Law and the prophets[133]. The radically changed life that we have received from Jesus has nothing whatsoever to do with the Law. The righteousness that we have now through the new birth is the absolute contrast to righteousness of Law-works[134]. The Law depended upon human ability, the righteousness by the faith of Jesus Christ is by the Holy

---

[129] (Jn. 15:1-7)
[130] (2 Pet. 1:3)
[131] (Eph. 4:24; Col. 3:10)
[132] (Jn. 10:18; Ac. 2:24; Rom. 8:11)
[133] (Rom. 3:22; 1 Pet. 1:11-12)
[134] (Gal. 2:16)

Spirit[135]. Through the faith of the Lord Jesus we were crucified together with Him and given His life. Now the life that we live, we live by the faith of Jesus[136]. It is impossible to separate righteousness by faith from the life that we have received in Christ Jesus. We are now found in Him, having His righteousness, which is the righteousness given to us when He gave us His life[137]. This is the righteousness of God given to us, not by the Law nor by Jewish traditions of righteousness that come by Law-works. It is by the faith of Jesus that we have boldness and access to God the Father and, even more, oneness with Him. It is by His righteousness that we come and are acceptable to the Father[138].

To understand that faith is not passive, but the working of God's supernatural power, we can examine how faith is introduced to us by Jesus. Faith first comes to light with respect to God's willingness and ability to provide in the most extraordinary way for His people[139]. God has invited us into a relationship of faith in which we "take no thought, saying, 'What shall we eat?' or, 'What shall we drink?' or, 'How shall we be clothed?'" He desires to teach us the principles of faith by setting our affections and interest solely on the Kingdom of God and His

---

[135] (Jn. 3:3-6; Rom. 8:1-3; 14:17)
[136] (Gal. 2:20)
[137] (Php. 3:9)
[138] (Eph. 1:6; 3:12; 1 Pet. 2:5; Rom. 15:16; Heb. 10:19)
[139] (Mt. 6:30)

righteousness[140]. Faith is taught to us on the basis of what we are persuaded that Jesus Christ will do for us if we will only believe. God shows us what great faith is by the example of the centurion who knew that Jesus had the power to heal his servant[141]. The Romans, who believed themselves to be the superior race, had a centurion who so honored Jesus that he did not feel worthy for Him to come into his house, but said "speak the word only" and I know my servant will be healed. Faith was all about what Jesus alone could do and the willingness of a person to believe in Him. Jesus demonstrated His power over the wind and the waves[142]. Everything that Jesus did was linked to faith. When anyone expressed confidence in His ability to heal or deliver, He called it faith. When He saw the faith of those who brought the paralytic to Him it was all that was needed for Jesus to speak forth the miracle "take up your bed and go home" (Mt. 9:2). When a woman came behind Him and touched his garment, her expectation of what Jesus could do was called faith[143]. Jesus described faith as the ability to move mountains and command trees to be pulled up by the roots and planted in the sea[144]. He described His ability to curse the fig tree, which immediately dried up, as faith and extended the same

---

[140] (Mt. 6:33; Col. 3:1-3; Heb. 11:14-16)
[141] (Mt. 8:10)
[142] (Mt. 8:26)
[143] (Mt. 9:22)
[144] (Mt. 17:20; 21:21)

ability to His disciples. Faith is all about believing what God has spoken and believing in those things that only God can do and what He will do for you. Faith is the release of the miracle power of God! Faith is not a mental assent or a passive religious posture before God. Faith is the power of God at work! And God's power is at work in all who believe[145].

---

[145] (Eph. 1:19; 3:20; 2 Cor. 4:7; 1 Cor. 2:5; Php. 2:13; Heb. 13:21)

Grace Through Righteousness Reigns

Grace reigns because the claims of sin and death were destroyed by the death, burial and resurrection of Jesus. This is the life that we have now been given because we were born again. When sin entered into the world condemnation passed upon all men. There was a promise given that man would be redeemed from the curse of sin. The Law entered to testify of the sin and death that ruled over humanity[146]. The Law was added until the Seed, Christ Jesus, should come. It testified to the condemnation and death sentence that was passed upon all men[147]. The Law testified to the sin that was in man. When Christ Jesus came, every sin and offense was removed by His blood for those who would receive His salvation. The reign of sin and death was destroyed by the death of Christ Jesus[148]. Grace testifies that the blood of Jesus which cleanses us from all sin now reigns. The washing of

---
[146] (Gal. 3:19-21)
[147] (Gen. 2:17; Rom. 5:12-21; 2 Cor. 3:9)
[148] (Heb. 2:14)

the water of regeneration now reigns. Every attribute of the triumph of Christ Jesus over sin and death now reigns. The grace that has come to us by Jesus reveals that we are washed, made holy, made righteous, in the name of the Lord Jesus and by the Spirit of our God[149]. When we were freed from the law of sin and death, the Law of Moses could no longer testify against us. The Law, that could only condemn, through its statutes and ordinances, was removed. Now the blood of Jesus testifies of our cleansing and His resurrection of our new life. The grace of God testifies that we have been made righteous. Sin has no more dominion and the righteousness of the Law is fulfilled in us who now walk after the Spirit[150].

Christ Jesus now reigns over our lives. What Jesus did for us and continues to do on our behalf is called Grace. By grace we are saved and that grace was accomplished by Jesus Christ who purchased our salvation[151]. Grace is fully comprehended in the death, burial, resurrection, ascension and reign of Jesus[152]. It was by grace that we were redeemed from all iniquity and made the workmanship of Christ created for good works[153]. The grace that brought salvation to us is personified in Christ Jesus. The grace that is now revealed comes to us by the

---

[149] (1 Cor. 6:11)
[150] (Rom. 8:1-4)
[151] (Jn. 1:17; Rom. 11:6)
[152] (Eph. 1:6-7; 2:8)
[153] (Eph. 2:8-10; Tt. 2:14)

Made Righteous by Faith

Holy Spirit. Grace lifts the standard of the kingdom and reign of Christ Jesus – teaching us to deny all ungodliness and worldly lust[154]. Grace is represented as the power of the Holy Spirit at work on the inside of us[155].

The grace of God and the reign of grace is comprehended in the change that has been brought to us by Jesus. In Adam all died but in Christ Jesus everyone who is born again is made alive. Through Adam's disobedience everyone was made sinners but through the obedience of Christ Jesus we were made righteous[156]. We inherited sin from Adam but we inherit righteousness from Christ Jesus. As we were born into this natural life under the rule of sin and death, we are born again into the rule of righteousness where Christ Jesus now reigns. The fall from fellowship with God was by Adam but our restoration to union with God is in Christ Jesus.

Adam passed a sin nature to his descendants[157]. Christ Jesus imparted the divine nature to those who trust in Him[158]. Adam brought death and condemnation, but Jesus brought life and righteousness[159]. Death reigned by Adam, but righteousness reigns by Jesus. And even more what Jesus has done for us is far more effective in our lives than

---

[154] (Tt. 2:11-12)
[155] (1 Cor. 15:10; Eph. 4:20; 6:10; 2 Cor. 4:7)
[156] (Rom. 5:19)
[157] (Rom. 5:12, 19; Eph. 2:3; Ps. 51:5)
[158] (Rom. 5:19; 2 Cor. 5:17–18; Tt. 3:5; 2 Pet. 1:4; Eph. 4:24)
[159] (Rom. 5:16–18; 3:24; 4:25; 1 Pet. 2:24)

what Adam did[160]. We were sinners before we ever sinned because of Adam's sin. But now much more we are righteous before there is any action of righteousness through Jesus Christ.

The working of the Grace of God does not mean that we are not held responsible for our actions. To say that sin has no impact on those made righteous in Christ Jesus contradicts 100's of scriptures. To say that righteousness did not have an impact on Noah or others who were righteous even though they were under the law of sin and death is equally wrong. Paul points out the spiritual blessings of the reign of grace in Romans 6. We are no longer under the power of sin and should never yield ourselves to its power. We are raised up with Christ Jesus and walking in the newness of His life. We now yield ourselves to God and our lives as instruments of righteousness. He underscores that sin still has a consequence but should have no dominion over us[161].

Sin did not come into the world by the Law, and the Law could not deliver anyone from it. Sin came by Adam's disobedience. Sin was removed by the redemption that is in Christ Jesus. When we are born again the testimony of the Law that condemns the nature of sin and death is no longer valid. He bore the sin away in His own body and removed the curse of sin and death revealed by the Law[162].

---

[160] (Rom. 5:15, 17, 20)
[161] (Rom. 6:1-2, 12-14, 15-16, 21, 23)
[162] (1 Pet. 2:24)

Made Righteous by Faith

Our sinful state was removed at the cross. The Law that testified against us was nailed to the tree when Christ Jesus was crucified[163]. Jesus destroyed the dominion of sin and the authority that Satan held over us[164]. Yet sin is still transgression against the Law; but now, through Christ Jesus, neither have dominion over us[165]. Now grace reigns through righteousness unto eternal life by Jesus Christ our Lord![166]

What did Paul mean when he said that where there is no law there is no transgression? First of all there was no Law of Moses in the days of Noah, but people were held responsible for their sins. There was no Law of Moses in the days of Sodom and Gomorrah, but the inhabitants were held responsible for their sin. Therefore, it would be a wrong conclusion to say that the removal of the Law of Moses takes away the consequence of sin. Sin has a consequence whether there is a Law of Moses or not. Paul underscores the responsibility that everyone has if they commit acts of sin as well as God's judgement against it many times. So what was Paul saying when he referred to those statements concerning the relationship of the Law to sin? What did he mean when he said:

- By the Law is the knowledge of sin.[167]

---

[163] (Col. 2:14-15)
[164] (Heb. 2:14; 2 Tim. 1:10; 1 Jn. 3:8)
[165] (1 Jn. 3:4; Rom. 6:14)
[166] (Rom. 5:21)
[167] (Rom. 3:20)

- Where there is no law there is no transgression.[168]
- Sin is imputed by the Law.[169]
- The Law entered that sin might be shown to be exceedingly sinful.[170]
- That the strength of sin is the law.[171]

Paul certainly was not saying that sin is no longer sinful. What he is saying is that the Law held everyone responsible for their sin and yet was powerless to deliver anyone from their sin. The Law shined a spotlight on sin but could not remove the sin. The judgment against sin was the wrath of God. Once again the Law could only establish the transgression of Adam's disobedience and could not remove it. When the Law was removed by the New Covenant in the blood of Jesus sin lost its dominion and there remained no more judgment.

The Law was not removed until Christ Jesus paid in full for the sin of man and brought in the New Covenant. The point that Paul was making is that the inheritance could not come by the Law. The law pointed to and proved their sinful condition. The faith of Jesus Christ brought the grace of God to us that delivered us from sin and death and established the promise. The most important thing to understand is that the New Covenant was established, fulfilling the promise made to Abraham.

---

[168] (Rom. 4:15)
[169] (Rom. 5:13)
[170] (Rom. 7:13)
[171] (1 Cor. 15:17)

Made Righteous by Faith

The Law brought the knowledge of sin to each person proving that they were sinners. It was by the Law that there was the knowledge of sin with no remedy – only condemnation. The Law identified men as sinners and separated from the life of God. There could be no real communion with God by the Law because it condemned men of the sins that they were held under. It was the Law that allowed us to understand those things that are evil and that are opposed to the ways of God[172]. The great statement of condemnation by the Law is "draw not nigh," for you are sinful[173]. The Law came so that the offence of sin against God might be abundantly evident[174]. Therefore no person could ever be shown to be righteous by the Law. The covenant of the Law was removed by the shed blood and resurrection of Jesus because the sin was removed. God now proves us to be righteous by His Son Jesus Christ and calls all men to draw near[175].

Those who would think for a minute that they are no longer responsible for their sin now that the law has been abolished would have to ignore the whole of the Bible that warns against sin and its consequences[176]. Just step back and ask yourself, "Why would God want to redeem us from sin? Is sin something that God would fellowship

---

[172] (Rom. 5:20; 7:7, 8:11, 13)
[173] (Ex. 3:5; Heb. 7:19)
[174] (Rom. 5:20)
[175] (Eph. 2:17-18; Heb. 10:1-2, 19-21; Rom. 8:1-3)
[176] (2 Pet. 2; Jude 1:3-19)

with now or in the future? Can sin be acceptable or agreeable to God? Perhaps if you dress it up and send it to church and give it some money to place in the offering then it is okay? Is the sin of a saint more tolerable than the sin of a sinner? Shall we rejoice that we can now sin and not be concerned about a possible judgment because we are not under the Law?" What we fail to realize is that God hates sin of any kind so much that He made Hell and an eternal judgment against it. If sin is acceptable in any form then shouldn't God repent for making Hell and just do away with it and any notion of judgment in the future? Could it be that the salvation that is in Christ Jesus delivered us from sin and its desires and liberated us to walk in the life of God[177].

The message of the Bible is that righteousness is far better than sin and that the ways of God are far better than the twisted nature of the Devil. Should we not rather rejoice that we have been delivered from the power of sin and are liberated to know God and the glorious realms of His abundant life. Why would we look for permission to hold on to sin after the message of salvation and liberation has come? What Paul would say to those who would think that that they could continue in sin because they are not under the law was, God forbid! Don't you realize that to whom you yield yourself you become its slave? If it is sin

---

[177] (1 Pet. 2:24; Rom. 6:1-23; 2 Cor. 5:17)

then you are slave to both sin and death[178]. Some would be so naïve as to suggest that Paul implied that we could sin without a consequence but nothing could be further from the truth. What Paul did say in light of this issue was,

> *"shall we continue in sin that grace may abound? No way! How can we who are dead to sin live any longer in it."*
>
> (Rom. 6:1-2)

Both the law and sin have been destroyed so that we can now serve God in righteousness and holiness all the days of our lives and worship Him in Spirit and in truth[179]. Paul was strongly opposed to any notion of those having been made righteous considering themselves sinners. Paul also made it clear that those who had come to faith in Christ Jesus could make themselves transgressors. He said, if while we seek to be made righteous by Christ we ourselves are found to be sinners then we in fact build again that which was destroyed and make ourselves transgressors[180]. Paul equated sin with the Law and the Law with sin insomuch that he argued that if you take away sin, you take away the need for the Law. What had to be destroyed first, the Law or the sin? Did Jesus come to destroy the Law? No, He came to destroy sin – and where

---
[178] (Rom. 6:15-16)
[179] (Lk. 1:74-75; Jn. 4:23)
[180] (Gal. 2:17-19)

there is no transgression, there is no need for a Law[181]. Paul argued that the life in Christ Jesus did not make the Law void, but rather established it[182]. How, because those who have been created anew in Christ Jesus and restored to a nature of righteousness and true holiness fulfill the righteousness of the law instinctively[183].

> "This doctrine seems liable to the imputation of licentiousness. St. Paul foresaw the objection, and answered it: his answer should satisfy every objector: but the reign of grace consists in destroying every effect of sin; therefore to indulge sin would be to counteract, and not to promote, the grace of God. Let the professors of religion however be careful to give no room for this objection: let them "put to silence the ignorance of foolish men by well-doing."
>
> (Charles Simeon, 1833)

"What he says, amounts to this nearly. What armed death against the world? The one man's eating from the tree only. If then death attained so great power from one offence, when it is found that certain received a grace and righteousness out of all proportion to that sin, how shall they still be liable

---

[181] (1 Tim. 1:9; 1 Jn. 3:4)
[182] (Rom. 3:31)
[183] (Rom. 8:4; Gal. 3:21; 5:14; Rom. 13:8, 10; Eph. 4:24; Heb. 8:10; 2 Cor. 3:3)

to death? And for this cause, he does not here say 'grace,' but 'superabundance of grace.' For it was not as much as we must have to do away the sin only, that we received of His grace, but even far more. For we were at once freed from punishment, and put off all iniquity, and were also born again from above (John 3:3) and rose again with the old man buried, and were redeemed, justified, led up to adoption, sanctified, made brothers of the only-begotten, and joint heirs and of one Body with Him, and counted for His Flesh, and even as a Body with the Head, so were we united unto Him! All these things then Paul calls a "superabundance" of grace, showing that what we received was not a medicine only to countervail the wound, but even health, and comeliness, and honor, and glory and dignities far transcending our natural state."

(John Chrysostom, 2nd Century AD)

Faith Works, not Law Works

"Yes, a man may say, 'You have faith, and I have works: show me your faith without your works, and I will show you my faith by my works.'"

(Jas. 2:18)

Paul refers to faith-works or the "works of God" in our lives 33 times, but many more times in an indirect way[184]. These are the works of Jesus Christ in our lives. The power of God at work in us, not human works. These are not works of self-righteousness or Law-works – these are the works of the Spirit in the lives of those who have been born again. Paul contrasts three kinds of works in Ephesians 2:8-10: The work of faith which brought to pass salvation – the washing of the water of regeneration (born again); The works which are Law-works – the Jews attempted to make themselves acceptable to God by the

---

[184] (Ac. 26:20; Rom. 2:15, 13:12; 1 Cor. 3:13-14, 15:58, 16:10; 2 Cor. 9:8, 11:15; Gal. 6:4; Eph. 2:10; Php. 2:12, 30; Col. 1:10, 29; 1 Thess. 1:3, 5:13; 2 Thess. 2:17; 1 Tim. 2:10, 5:10, 25, 6:18; 2 Tim. 2:21, 3:17; Tt. 1:16, 2:7, 14, 3:1, 8, 14; Heb. 6:10, 10:24, 13:21)

Law. Finally, the works of God – God's work, by which we were created anew in Christ Jesus. This is the work of faith which is the product of God's workmanship. He created us anew to live His life – to bring forth the works of God by the working of the Holy Spirit, which He ordained that we should walk in, these are faith-works[185].

Faith-works are the works that only God can do through our lives. Faith-works are the working of the Holy Spirit in us, thus works of the Spirit. The Holy Spirit brings to us everything that Jesus is doing as His faith operates through our lives[186]. Faith takes the highest place in the New Testament because New Testament faith is all about the finished work of Jesus. Everything that we do in Christ Jesus is by faith. The miraculous work of faith all begins with the transformation of our lives, from that which is flesh to that which is Spirit[187]. We were born of the Spirit to live and walk in the Spirit. The Holy Spirit supplies to us that which mere flesh and blood could never do. The Law was weak not only because it could not impart the life of God, but also because it depended upon the ability of men[188]. Faith-works are the works of the Holy Spirit in our lives, whereas Law-works are the works of an unredeemed man attempting to be made righteous by his own human

---

[185] (Eph 2:10; Col. 1:10)
[186] (Ac. 3:16; Jn. 16:13-15)
[187] (Jn. 3:3-6; Rom. 8:9)
[188] (Gal. 3:21; Rom. 8:3; Heb. 7:18)

effort. Faith-works are: Christ in us and His life lived out through our lives by the Holy Spirit.

As we have said, faith in the Old Testament was all about the coming Seed, the one who would redeem mankind. The faith that Paul described in the New Testament is found in the results of what Christ Jesus has brought to pass, the re-creation of our lives[189]. Faith is one of the most important and powerful words in the Bible. There is only one faith, and that faith is given to us in a relationship with the only true God and His Son Jesus Christ. Faith is introduced to us in the Gospels as the power that only Jesus Christ has that is now expressed both to us and through us because He is in us. Faith is revealed in the lives of men as they recognize Who Christ Jesus is and what He alone can do.

Faith is all about the relationship that men are willing to have with God. Those who are willing know Him and live for Him. Those who are willing to believe what He says and obey[190]. It is by this obedience to God's Word that we understand faith-works. The Holy Spirit empowers the Word of God in the person who obeys, and faith-works are demonstrated as the supernatural power of God at work in our lives. When faith was demonstrated through the life of Jesus, God brought Heaven to Earth, and man beheld the greatest power of God that humanity

---

[189] (Eph. 4:24; Col. 3:10; 2 Cor. 5:17; Tt. 3:5)
[190] (Heb. 11:28-35)

had ever seen. Jesus modeled for us what faith-works look like. He showed us that faith-works come by doing the will of the Father.

Paul also describes faith-works by the demonstration of the Holy Spirit and power. He described faith-works as mighty signs and wonders. He described faith as a gift of the Spirit and as a fruit of the Spirit. He described it as God at work within him. The ability to walk with God, to work righteousness, as the power to "remove mountains," and so much more. God desires for all of us to walk in these faith-works. We were born again to live the life of Jesus. We received power from on High to be a witness of the power of Jesus. The Gospel is to be preached with these faith-works that are the demonstration of the Spirit. The religious Law-works of the Jews could never arise to the kind of works that God desires for our lives. Our hearts desire should be that God would count us,

> *"... worthy of the calling and fulfill all the goodness of His good pleasure and work of faith in power, so that the name of our Lord Jesus Christ will be glorified in you, and you in Him, according to the grace of our God and the Lord Jesus Christ."*
>
> (2 Thess. 1:11–12)

This was the case not only with Paul, but also with Stephen and everyone else in the New Testament who demonstrated the life and power of the faith of Jesus[191]. These are the works of God's people – works of faith and power. The works of the redeemed are love, joy, peace, and all the rest of the fruits of righteousness. Every demonstration of the life of God in us is a faith-work.

It is God who does these faith works. These faith-works have no limits, and are the expressions of Christ in us. It's His life in us that gives us the ability to do His works and greater works[192]. All these faith-works are a witness to His life in us[193]. They are the works of the Spirit. They are observed in every dimension of life as fruits of the Spirit and demonstrations of power. They are demonstrated as gifts of revelation, gifts of power and gifts of utterance[194]. They are works of righteousness and the manner of the life of God in us. They are the works that Jesus did, who went about doing good and healing all who were oppressed of the Devil[195]. They are the fruits of His life, the works of righteousness.

Law-works are understood in the New Testament as those works that a person does in an unregenerate state, attempting to establish their own righteousness. Paul summarizes Law-works when he referred to the rebellious Jews of His day as

---

[191] (Ac. 3:16; 6:5, 8; 11:24; 14:9, etc.)
[192] (Jn. 14:12; Gal. 5:23)
[193] (1 Jn. 4:13, 17)
[194] (1 Cor. 7:11)
[195] (Ac. 10:45)

> *"...being ignorant of God's righteousness, and going about to establish their own righteousness, have not submitted themselves unto the righteousness of God."*
>
> (Rom. 10:3)

Those who trusted in the Law for righteousness never attained the righteousness of God because they rejected Jesus. They rejected His word. They rejected the faith, the faith of the New Covenant, and therefore the new birth[196]. Righteousness could never come by the Law, because the Law could not impart the life of God[197]. The Jews had created all kinds of traditions around the Law and made it about attaining righteousness, rather than their need for the coming Redeemer. The Law could never make someone righteous – it only proved that men were unrighteous and bound by sin[198]. The very definition of self-righteousness is a person attempting to be acceptable to God through the works of the Law[199]. Law-works were powerless in every way. They could never result in righteousness nor demonstrate any dimension of the living presence of the Living God.

The Law could never impart the life of Christ Jesus. The Law could not result in anyone being born of the Holy Spirit. True righteousness could never come by the Law[200].

---

[196] (Rom. 9:30-32)
[197] (Gal. 3:21)
[198] (Rom. 7:13; Gal. 2:16; 3:10, 13; 2 Cor. 3:9; Rom. 4:15)
[199] (Php. 3:9; Rom. 10:3)
[200] (2 Cor. 13:5; Php. 1:11; 2 Cor. 3:3)

The manifestations of Christ in us are faith-works. We were created by Christ Jesus for good works – these are not Law-works[201]. We were purified and made righteous by the new birth to be zealous for good works: His works through our lives[202]. If Christ Jesus is in us, then the life that we now live in the flesh will reveal His life[203]. If we are led by the Spirit, then the life of the Spirit will be manifested through us. As many as are led by the Spirit are not under the Law. As many as are led – who live the life of the Holy Spirit – are the sons of God[204].

---

[201] (2 Cor. 13:5; Eph. 2:10)
[202] (Tt. 2:14)
[203] (2 Cor. 13:5; Gal. 2:20; 5:18; Php. 1:20; Col. 3:3-4; Rom. 6:4; 8:2, 14; 2 Cor. 4:11 etc.)
[204] (Gal. 5:22-25; Rom. 7:4)

Made the Righteousness of God in Him

"For He has made Him to be sin for us, Who knew no sin; that we might be made the righteousness of God in Him."

(2 Cor. 5:21)

The Lord Jesus moved us far beyond any concept of righteousness that the Jewish community might have thought possible to be obtained through the Law. The righteousness of God, which the Law could have never given, is now ours for the asking. Both the Law and the prophets foretold of this glorious realm, but it was not something available to them[205]. God made His righteousness available to sinful man on the basis of believing in Jesus, repenting, and confessing Him as Lord. As many as would receive Him He gave them the

---

[205] (Rom. 3:21; 1 Pet. 1:11-12; Jn. 5:46; Ac. 26:22)

authority to be the sons of God[206]. All that is necessary is for a person to believe and the new beginning comes by the power of the Holy Spirit.

The righteousness of God was given to us by the resurrection of Jesus from the dead. The righteousness of God was given to us when we were created anew in Christ Jesus[207]. The righteousness of God was given to us because He made us a new creation in Himself. The righteousness of God came into us because Christ Jesus dwells in us and we in Him. There is nothing that speaks louder of the power of God at work in us than to understand that Christ Jesus is in us and we in Him. The righteousness of God was given to us because Christ Jesus came into our lives when He gave us His life. The righteousness of God came into us because His Holy Spirit came into us. God not only imputed righteousness, He imparted His righteousness by His very life, thus giving us the power to do righteousness by the Spirit[208]. Every dimension of His goodness stepped into our lives when He created us anew in Himself. God made Him to be our righteousness, our holiness, and our redemption. The prophet Jeremiah said concerning the new covenant that God the Father would be called our righteousness, "The LORD our righteousness"(יְהוָ֥ה צִדְקֵֽנוּ׃, 'Yehovah sed-kenu')[209]. When we were made a

---
[206] (Jn. 1:12)
[207] (Eph. 2:6, 10; Rom. 6:4)
[208] (Rom. 1:8-9; 6:11; 14:17; 1 Pet. 2:24; Php. 1:11)
[209] (Jer. 23:6)

new creation, God not only made Jesus to be our righteousness – He Himself became our righteousness.

Paul had passionately sought for righteousness through the Law. He had given his whole life to understand the righteousness that comes by keeping the Law. He was a Pharisee of the Pharisees who, concerning the Law, had a great zeal. Everything changed for Paul when He met Jesus on the road to Damascus, for when He met Jesus, he met righteousness. Christ Jesus gave to Paul what he had sought to have through the merit of the Law but could never attain. He, in an instant, received the righteousness of God through the new birth. Everything was different for him from that moment on. He received the righteousness that only belongs to God when Christ Jesus stepped into his life. He no longer needed the Law for righteousness, for He had been given God's own righteousness and the power of it.

Mankind was in this world without God and without hope[210]. There was no one who had the righteousness that God desired for mankind. Even more, there was no one who had the ability to establish God's righteousness in their lives. How can it be that God could instantly take a sinful man and make him righteous? What great miracle can take place that all the sin that men have committed could be forever removed? God showed us, throughout the Law, over and again, how He would remove the sin

---

[210] (Eph. 2:12)

and make a person innocent through the thousands of sacrifices offered for sin. All of those sacrifices were to point to the one sacrifice that God would make. It was supposed to have been a ritual and daily reminder of the coming redeemer but few saw it. Still, God came and was made the sacrifice for sin. God transferred all our sins to Jesus, while at the same time transferring Christ Jesus' righteousness to us. The One who knew no sin became for us our sin offering that we might be made the righteousness of God in Him.[211]

Many may think, surely there is something that I must do? How can it be that easy? How can I lay claim to something that I do not deserve? How can it be possible that God, Who truly is in every way righteous and has never done anything that is wrong, would supply me with His own righteousness? All these things that God has done do not need to be understood by the reason of men, for they are the revelation of the Father. If men choose to live by their reason and what they think they deserve, then the revelation of God will never be accepted. Until we will agree with the living word of God, we will not know the great miracle which He works by it. It is not for us to sit and judge whether God's word is true or not, but to agree with what He has said and rejoice in what He has done. All our iniquities were laid upon Christ Jesus. He was wounded for our transgressions and bruised for our

---

[211] (2 Cor. 5:21)

iniquities. Surely He has borne our sorrows and by His stripes we were healed. He was made the sin-offering for us that we may be made γενώμεθα ('genometha') the righteousness of God in Him in an instant – in a moment – when we are born again. Being "made" ('genometha') righteous is very different from having been "credited" (λογίζομαι, 'logizomai') righteousness!

Christ Jesus was the Passover Lamb without spot or blemish. He was the goat-offering of atonement to which all our sins were transferred. He was the ram-offering for sin, which was offered to satisfy the punishment for our iniquity. He was the guilt offering that took away all our shame. In every conceivable way sin and condemnation was removed and God's righteousness established. Yet God did not stop there. He empowered us with His own life to live out the life He redeemed us for. He imparted His righteousness to us so that we might be conformed to His image and be as He is[212]. His righteousness is in us because He is in us[213]. The sacrifice God made for our sins would not be as the one offered to cover the nakedness of Adam and Eve, but to cleanse and wash away all sin by the death of His Son. He would not clothe us with the skins of those offerings that were slain, but instead clothe us with His righteousness. It would not be just an outward change, but He would wipe clean the inward man. Our lives would

---

[212] (Rom. 8:29; 1 Jn. 4:17)
[213] (1 Jn. 3:24; 4:4)

not be just a tent set up in the wilderness for Him to tabernacle in, but He would fill the tent of our lives with His glory, and place us in His heavenly realm.

The reformers made a terrible mistake: they never grasped the reality of union with Christ Jesus. The message of Jesus in the gospel of John never became a part of their concept of justification by faith. They were confused about what merit based righteousness was all about. They limited the whole message of righteousness by faith to Romans 3-4, and Galatians 2-3, which did not fully reveal the union with Christ Jesus and His imparted righteousness. It was for this reason that antinomianism was a short step away from their concept of justification by faith. They were unable to realize and accept that Christ Jesus is in us and we are in Him. The reality of the Holy Spirit being both with us and in us did not find a place in their doctrine, which placed constraints and limits on the ability to do righteousness by the indwelling power of God. They limited the righteousness of God to only a legal status before God and not a supernatural change of the new creation which is Christ in us.

Made the Righteousness of God in Him by the Faith of Jesus Christ

"Knowing that a man is not made righteous by the works of the Law but by the faith of Jesus Christ, even we have believed in Jesus Christ, that we might be made righteous by the faith of Christ for by the works of the Law no flesh shall be made righteous."

(Gal. 2:16)

The faith of Jesus Christ is expressed in all that Jesus did and all that He continues to do for us. He has given us His righteousness that has nothing to do with who we are and what we have done. Rather, all we need to do is believe, a believing that brings forth His righteousness through the new birth. The Faith of Jesus Christ made us a new creation, thereby giving us His righteousness, His power at work in us. Adam was created from the fine dust of the earth, but we were created new in Christ Jesus[214]. Both the Law and the prophets testified of the New Covenant that would bring into being a new beginning for man. Many prophets and righteous men saw the glory of the new creation by the Spirit, even though they were not able to partake of it[215]. Now it is revealed- its the new creation in which all things are made new!

The faith of Jesus Christ is discovered in what He accomplished. God the eternal Word became the Captain of our salvation[216]. Jesus was manifested to destroy the works of darkness[217]. He through His death destroyed the one who had the power of death: the Devil[218]. He brought life and immortality to light through the Gospel[219]. He rose up from the dead and brought resurrection life to each one of us by His own power[220]. He gave gifts unto men and divided the spoils with the strong[221]. He purchased our salvation with His own blood[222]. He received the Holy Spirit from the Father and poured it out upon all flesh[223]. He brought to us the power to be translated from the kingdom of this world into His

---

[214] (Eph. 2:10; Col 3:10)
[215] (1 Pet. 1:12; Dan. 12:9; Heb. 11:39-40; Mt. 13:17)
[216] (Heb. 2:10, 12:2; Ac. 20:26; Isa. 53:12; 59:16)
[217] (1 Jn. 3:8)
[218] (Heb. 2:14)
[219] (2 Tim. 1:10)
[220] (Jn. 10:18; Col. 2:12; 3:1-3; Eph. 2:6)
[221] (Eph. 4:11; Isa. 53:12)
[222] (Ac. 20:28; 1 Pet. 2:1; Rev. 1:5; 5:9; 7:14)
[223] (Ac. 2:33; Jn. 7:39)

Kingdom[224]. He made us not of this world just as He is not of this world[225]. He gave us the spiritual circumcision which removed the sins of the flesh[226].

Jesus was manifested to take away sin, and in Him is no sin[227]. The great wonder of God's amazing grace is that we are in Him and He is in us by what Jesus did for us and continues to do in us. By His faith and by His intercession we are saved to the utmost[228]. We are kept by His power and perfected by His works. It was by His faith that Father gave us His glory and made us one with Himself[229].

The Law was not the promise – Jesus was the promise. There was no power contained within the Law to change the heart and spirit of men. The Law had no ability to bring to pass the promise made to Abraham. However, the faith of Jesus Christ, Who loved us and gave Himself for us, did. God was incarnated into the likeness of sinful flesh to work the miracle of the new creation. It was by His obedience that we were given the opportunity to be made a new creation and thereby be made righteous. It's only because He came, as a babe in a manger, that we can be born of the Spirit. It was because He laid aside His glory that we can now have His glory in our lives[230]. He paid the

---
[224] (Col. 1:13)
[225] (Jn. 17:14, 16)
[226] (Col. 2:11)
[227] (1 Jn. 3:8)
[228] (Heb. 7:25; Col. 2:10)
[229] (Jn. 17:21-23; 14:17,21-23)
[230] (Jn. 17:22; Col. 1:27; 2 Thess. 1:12)

price for us to receive His life dwelling in us. Through His life and sacrifice He was given the Holy Spirit to pour out upon us[231]. He paid a great price for us to have His life in full – we should embrace all of it[232]. If we believe that Christ Jesus dwells in us, then we should believe that His life will be manifested through us. We now live this life in the flesh by His faith[233].

Christ Jesus dwells in our hearts by faith, and that's the faith of the new covenant, the faith of Jesus Christ[234]. The faith of Jesus is described by all that Jesus said and did. Yet most importantly the faith of the New Covenant is the miracle of the new birth, that brought forth the life of Christ Jesus in us. We were bought with the price of the blood of Jesus. He is now to be glorified in our bodies and spirits[235]. It's His life we are to live, not our own. It's His faith that we are to live by, not our own, for truly He is the faith and the faith is by Him.

The curse of the Law of Moses no longer exists; it was put to death at the cross. The legal system and its ordinances were blotted out[236]. There was no life imparting power in them. In the unregenerate state, it could only condemn[237]. Now through the righteousness

---

[231] (Ac. 2:33; Jn. 14:26)
[232] (Jn. 1:16; Col. 2:9-10)
[233] (Gal. 2:20)
[234] (Eph. 3:17)
[235] (1 Cor. 6:20)
[236] (Eph. 2:15; Col. 2:14)
[237] (2 Cor. 3:9)

that comes by faith we are able to fulfill the righteousness of the Law[238]. We do not live by the Law, but we live by every word that proceeds from the mouth of God[239]. We have the life of God in us like a well spring and rivers flowing from our inner being. We have the life of the Holy Spirit, the eternal life of God. It is by His word and by His Spirit that the righteous live by faith. We live by the faith of Jesus who brought forth this new existence. We live by believing everything that God has spoken. We live in a new beginning that has come and that new beginning is in Christ Jesus. He is the new and living way and it's only through His life that we can live[240]. He died and rose again that we might live, and in Him is life and righteousness.

Because of Adam's disobedience we were **made** sinners, but by the obedience of Christ Jesus we were **made** righteous[241]. Being made righteous (δικαιοι κατασταθησονται, 'dikaioi katastathēsontai') is not the same as being counted righteous (λογίζεται δικαιοσύνην, 'logizetai dikaiosynēn')[242]. Just as we were caused to be (καθίστημι, 'kathistemi') sinners because of Adam's disobedience, we were caused to be ('kathistemi') righteous by the obedience of Jesus. We certainly had the deeds of sin produced in our lives because of Adam's

---

[238] (Rom. 8:4; 13:8, 10; Mt. 5:17; Gal. 5:14)
[239] (Mt. 4:4; Deut. 8:3)
[240] (Heb. 10:20)
[241] (Rom. 5:19)
[242] (Rom. 4:6, 22-24)

disobedience. How could it ever be said that – having been <u>caused to be</u> righteous through the obedience of Christ Jesus – we would not have the deeds of righteousness now manifested in our lives?

> *"For He has <u>made</u> Him to be sin for us, Who knew no sin, that we might be <u>made</u> the righteousness of God in Him.*
>
> (2 Cor. 5:21)

Yet again, we see that <u>γίνομαι</u> ('ginomai', "made") is not a synonym for λογίζομαι ('logizomai', "count"). The Greek word ginomai is a word used to describe being born or "to come into being." Being made righteous is the transformation that took place when we were born again, in which we actually became righteous! We were made, or became, the righteousness of God through the grace brought to us by Jesus Christ[243]. Neither 'kathistemi' ("caused to be") nor 'ginomai' ("made") are synonyms with 'logizetai' ("counted"). **Paul is speaking of two different realities.** Because we were willing to believe the Word of God and agree with Him concerning redemption in His Son, we were counted righteous. However, Paul did not leave it there, because unlike Abraham and all Old Testament saints, we were born again! We were made a new creation – they were not. We do not just have a legal status of righteousness in Christ Jesus, but we are also

---

[243] (2 Cor. 5:21; 1 Cor. 1:30; Eph. 2:8-10)

made the righteousness of God because He was made (became) the sin-offering for us. There is nothing that could speak more loudly of a substance change. We have been given the divine nature, a new spirit and a new heart[244]. The old is gone and the new has come so that we might walk in the newness of life[245]. We were not just born of the flesh– we were born of the Spirit and now we are Spirit[246]. As real as we were born of our earthly parents, we were also born of God! As real as He bore our sins in His own body, we were empowered to live unto righteousness[247]. Our lives are now hidden in Christ Jesus. We now live by Him just as a branch lives by the vine. We are crucified with Christ, buried together, raised together, alive together, and seated together in a heavenly realm. His life is our life!

---

[244] (2 Pet. 1:4; Jn. 3:3; 2 Cor. 5:17)
[245] (Rom. 6:5)
[246] (Rom. 8:9; Jn. 3:5-6)
[247] (1 Pet. 2:24)

Can Faith Alone Make Righteous?

"You see then how by works a man is shown righteous, and not by faith only."

(Jas. 2:24)

When James refers to "faith alone" he is speaking of faith that does not result in the change of a person's manner of life[248]. He's referring to an acknowledgment of truth without the miracle of transformation. James also cites Abraham as a source for what he said, just as Paul did. Were James and Paul contradicting each other? Or is there a way to understand what they said without a contradiction? Both James and Paul are testifying of the power of faith that transforms a person's life. Faith that does not transform a person is dead just as the body without the spirit is dead. Paul tells us about the faith that makes one righteous and James is speaking specifically of the evidence of the transformation that came by faith. When a person is made a new creation they live by the

---

[248] (Jas. 2:24)

Spirit and the works of the Spirit are revealed. This is the more specific terminology used by Paul, who speaks of the transformation in terms of the works of the Spirit.

Paul and James are speaking on the basis of the same authority. They were both given the commission to reveal God's Word to His church. James is not making works the means by which a person is made righteous, but instead is underscoring the change that is brought about *because* a person has been made righteous. James is referring to the same works that every voice in the New Testament referred to, including Jesus[249]. James is not saying that a person is made righteous by works –we can be certain that James believed that a person is made righteous by faith. Rather, what he is saying is that if a person is made righteous by faith, then his life will demonstrate that righteousness[250].

Paul describes righteousness that comes by faith on the basis of Abraham's faith in the coming Seed, Who was Christ[251]. James is not denying faith in Jesus alone for righteousness. Instead, he is highlighting the obedience of the life of Christ in those who are born of the Spirit and have been made righteous. He proves this by showing that Abraham's righteousness was demonstrated by his obedience. Abraham's obedience to God was the most

---

[249] (Mt. 5:16; 16:27; Eph. 2:10; 1 Tim. 6:18; 2 Tim. 3:17; Tt. 1:16, 2:7, 14; 3:8)
[250] (Jas. 2:14–26)
[251] (Gen. 15:6)

radical of all in the Old Testament. In obedience to God, he offered Isaac as a human sacrifice[252]. James revealed that when Abraham was obedient, God showed him to be righteous[253]. (If Abraham's righteousness can result in such a radical display of obedience, then the argument would hold that we can certainly show acts of love to one another.) James further applies Abraham's obedience to the reason that he was called the friend of God[254]. James said in no uncertain terms that without works, faith is dead, being alone[255]. James is underscoring the transformative work of faith, because faith is accompanied by works. The faith that makes a person righteous brings about a change of life and conduct. Faith that makes righteous also results in the works of righteousness. Therefore, James says it is by works that a man is revealed to be righteous[256]. James makes faith dead without works in the same way that a body is dead without the spirit[257].

> *"Abraham believed in the promised Seed, 'in whom all the nations of the earth should be blessed.' But what kind of faith? Was it unproductive of holy obedience? No: it led him to obey the hardest command that was ever given to mortal man, even to*

---

[252] (Gen. 22:12)
[253] (Jas. 2:21; Gen. 15:6; 22:12)
[254] (Jas. 2:23; 2 Chr. 20:7; Isa. 41:8)
[255] (Jas. 2:17)
[256] (Jas. 2:24)
[257] (Jas. 2:26)

slay, and to reduce to ashes upon the altar, that very son, to whom the promises were made, and through whom alone they could ever be accomplished."
(Charles Simeon, 1833)

James is most definitely referring to a faith that is more than a mental assent, more than a passive acknowledgment, but instead a power so transformative that it results in a change of life. We possess the extraordinary life of God therefore it will be evident! Faith without the action of doing what is right is merely a mental acknowledgment that is no different than the belief that demons have[258]. James is underscoring that believing alone is not enough. Paul certainly was of the same mind, as we previously pointed out, he describes works in the believer's life 33 different times. To think that Paul did not look at faith as more than a passive or mental assent is certainly wrong. Paul described the transformative power of faith in terms of the life of Jesus in us. He focused on the new creation, the Son of God revealed in our lives by the working of the Holy Spirit in us and through us[259]. Paul characterized faith that declares a person righteous, as faith that produces the fruits of righteousness[260]. The chief characteristic of righteousness by faith is the love of God and the works of His love in our lives.

---

[258] (Jas. 2:19)
[259] (Gal. 1:16; Eph. 1:19; 3:20; 2 Cor. 4:7)
[260] (Php. 1:11; Eph. 5:9; Heb. 12:11)

When Paul was writing about Abraham's righteousness it was solely on the basis of Abraham's faith in the coming Seed[261]. James writes about the test of that righteousness that took place many years later[262]. James underscores that Abraham's righteousness was found to be "<u>perfected</u>" (<u>ἐτελειώθη</u>, 'eteleiothe') in his willingness to be perfectly obedient to God[263]. Therefore, James says that Abraham was shown to be righteous when God said, "Now I know that you fear me" (Gen. 22:12). Yet at the same time, James uses the plural form of works (ἔργοις, 'ergois') when describing Abraham's obedience (vs. 22). We certainly have many great examples of Abraham's obedience to God beginning in Genesis 12:1. However it cannot be underscored enough that Paul too described faith in action as the works of righteousness[264]. Paul is against the doctrine of works-based salvation – specifically Law-works. The works that James is referring to are not works that make righteous – these are the deeds of those who are *already made* righteous by faith and as a result have faith-works. At the same time, both James and Paul are opposed to the mere profession of faith that did not bring a

---

[261] (Gen. 15:6; John 8:56; Gal. 3:16; cr. Rom. 4:3; Gal. 3:6)
[262] (Gen. 22:1)
[263] (Jas. 2:22)
[264] (Ac. 26:20; Rom. 2:15; 13:12; 1 Cor. 3:13-14; 15:58; 16:10; 2 Cor. 9:8; 11:15; Gal. 6:4; Eph. 2:10; Php. 2:12, 30; Col. 1:10, 29; 1 Thess. 1:3; 5:13; 2 Thess. 2:17; 1 Tim. 2:10; 5:10, 25; 6:18; 2 Tim. 2:21; 3:17; Tt. 1:16; 2:7, 14; 3:1, 8, 14; Heb. 6:10; 10:24; 13:21)

Made Righteous by Faith

transformation of life. Why? It is simply because New Testament faith is to be born again.

Both James and Paul make it clear that faith comes as a result of the Word of God[265]; the Word of God that Peter proclaimed we are begotten of[266]; the Word of God that we are to live by[267]; the Word that brings forth faith. The faith of Jesus (the Living Word) produced the supernatural works of God in our lives. God's faith set in motion the action of believing.

Faith-works can never be equated with Law-works, for one is the work of God, and the other is the work of man. Faith-works come only through those who have been made righteous by faith through the new birth, whereas Law-works are a vain attempt to become righteous in an unregenerate state. It is only through Christ Jesus and His redeeming blood that anyone can be made righteous. We were made right by the mercies of God so that we can do what is right. Christ Jesus came into our lives so that He can be revealed through our lives. We were not made right to continue to do wrong[268].

---

[265] (Jas. 1:21; Rom. 10:17)
[266] (1 Pet. 1:23)
[267] (Deut. 8:3, Ps. 119:116, Mt. 4:4)
[268] (Rom. 1:18; 3:15; 6:1, 6, 16; Gal 5:19-21, 24-25)

Everlasting Righteousness

"...to finish the transgression, and to make an end of sins, and to make reconciliation for iniquity, and to bring in everlasting righteousness."

(Dan. 9:24)

Daniel prophesied of the coming Redeemer and said that He would bring in everlasting righteousness[269]. The Kingdom of God is the Kingdom of everlasting righteousness[270]. Christ Jesus was crowned King of the Kingdom almost 2,000 years ago. This is the kingdom that we seek and also the kingdom that we live in by the Spirit[271]. The church is the revelation of the kingdom of God on earth. Christ Jesus the King is the Head of the church. The church is His body, and the Kingdom belongs to us now as well as in the future[272]. His Kingdom of everlasting righteousness is revealed as we shine with His

---

[269] (Dan. 9:24)
[270] (Ps. 119:142)
[271] (Mt. 6:33; Col. 1:13; Eph. 2:6)
[272] (Mt. 5:3, 10)

light which is the light of His righteousness. The church, His body, is supposed to reveal the fullness of Who He is[273].

The Apostle Peter described the New Heaven and the New Earth as the places where righteousness dwells[274]. The new creation that we now are in Christ Jesus is the firstfruits of His eternal kingdom of righteousness. The Psalmist said that the righteous shall be the ones that inherit this land and dwell there forever[275]. The righteous shall shine as the stars forever[276]. There will be everlasting righteousness because God's throne is forever and ever and all that He is and does is in righteousness. He is the One who created all things and sustains all things and He loves righteousness and hates iniquity[277]. Those who will live and reign with Him forever will live with the One Who is righteous, loves righteousness, and beholds the face of those who do right[278]. All who reign with Him shall be clothed in righteousness[279]. God sits upon the throne of His holiness forever, and righteousness expresses His holiness. Righteousness and holiness not only describes His throne and how He reigns forever but describes the essence of His rulership[280]. God has reigned

---

[273] (Mt. 5:14; Eph. 1:23; Php. 2:15)
[274] (2 Pet. 3:13; Isa. 65:7)
[275] (Ps. 37:29)
[276] (Dan. 12:3)
[277] (Ps. 45:6)
[278] (Ps. 11:7)
[279] (Ps. 132:9; Isa. 61:10; Rev. 19:8)
[280] (Ps. 89:14; 97:2)

in righteousness for all eternity and will continue to reign in righteousness for all eternity to come. God reigns in righteousness now and those who represent Him and reign with Him show forth His righteousness. His kingdom is a kingdom of righteousness now and forevermore. It is this kingdom and righteousness that we are to seek and live for[281]. Our spirits have been made one with the Spirit of the Lord and if we are willing we can move with Him in all things that He Himself is doing.

The Holy Spirit desires to lead us in the paths of righteousness for His name's sake. We were born into His everlasting righteousness when we were born again. We were translated into the kingdom of Jesus Christ[282]. We are reigning in this life with Him and are seated together with Him in the heavenly realm[283]. We should desire to live our lives today just as we will live them throughout eternity. At the heart of this is our will. There will never be anything different about our will in heaven than it is right now today on Earth. If we have been born of God, then it should be our desire for our Heavenly Father's will to be done now just as it is in Heaven. The Spirit of the Son that we have now received is one that desires to do only the will of the Father[284]. Righteousness is the expression of all God's ways, and as His children we should want to learn

---

[281] (Mt. 6:33; Col. 1:13)
[282] (Col. 1:13)
[283] (Eph. 2:16; Rom. 5:17)
[284] (Gal. 4:6; Jn. 5:19-20)

them. Sin has no more dominion over us, so why should we want to yield our lives to sin?

> *"No weapon that is formed against us shall prosper; And every tongue that shall rise against us in judgment we shall condemn. This is the heritage of the servants of the LORD, and their righteousness is of me," says the LORD."*
>
> (Isa. 54:17)

The righteousness that we have of God stands up against every opposing force that works against the will of God. God has made us His servants, the servants of righteousness[285]. Righteousness now reigns, and God has empowered us to live in the reign with Him in His righteousness.

Righteousness can never be confused with a life of sin. We cannot claim that we are the righteousness of God and continue to live in sin. Righteousness is the opposite of sin which is proved by hundreds of scriptures. Even Pharaoh recognized that the LORD was righteous and that he in contrast was the one who sinned[286]. This contrast is recognized and repeated many times throughout Scripture. It is an unmistakable contrast. The most dominant synonyms of sin are: evil, wickedness, and iniquity. Combined together as a contrast against

---

[285] (Rom. 6:18)
[286] (Ex. 9:27)

righteousness, they occur 340 times in the Bible. The New Testament makes the same emphasis as the Old Testament. The contrast of righteousness and sin are the same as the contrast of good and evil, light and darkness or truth and lie. It's the same as referring to right and wrong, they will never be equal in any way. Righteousness is an expression of a person's deeds just as much in the New Testament as it is in the Old Testament. The same description is given by Peter that was given by the Psalmist,

> *"For the eyes of the Lord are over the **righteous**, and his ears are open unto their prayers: but the face of the Lord is against them who do **evil**."*
>
> (1 Pet. 3:12; Ps. 34:15)

John says if we say that we have fellowship with Him and walk in darkness we lie and do not do the truth[287].

Once again, the unfruitful works of darkness are sin and are in opposition to righteousness[288]. Sin reigned and produced sin in our lives, now righteousness reigns and produces righteousness in our lives[289]. We are servants of righteousness, living under the ministry of righteousness[290]. We must awake to righteousness and sin

---

[287] (1 Jn. 1:6)
[288] (Eph. 5:11)
[289] (Rom. 5:21; 6:16-22)
[290] (Rom. 6:13, 16, 18, 20; 2 Cor. 3:9)

not![291] We should now be dead to sin and live out our lives under the reign of King Jesus in righteousness[292]. The most important thing of all to grasp about these two opposing ways of life are the words of Jesus:

> "And these shall go away into everlasting punishment, but the righteous into life eternal."
>
> (Mt. 25:46)

Righteousness is the light that shines from us into a dark world around us. It is the witness of a resurrected life and shows forth the life of Jesus in us.[293] Righteousness is the work of grace expressed through us as His workmanship[294]. Righteousness is expressed as the love of God, which is the evidence of being born of God. It is the gift of righteousness and the reign of righteousness that causes us to be fruitful in every good work[295]. There will either be the works of righteousness through the working of the Holy Spirit or we will show ourselves disobedient and absent of every good work[296]. When we were made the righteousness of God, we put off the former lifestyle ἀναστροφή ('anastrophe') and we were clothed with a new lifestyle[297]. Now our conduct should represent Christ

---

[291] (1 Cor. 15:34)
[292] (1 Pet. 2:24)
[293] (Mt. 5:14; Jn. 8:12; 1 Jn. 1:7; 2 Thess. 2:17; 2 Tim. 2:21, 3:17; Tt. 2:7, 3:1, 8, 14; Heb. 10:24; 13:21; 1 Pet. 2:12 etc.)
[294] (Eph. 2:10)
[295] (Col. 1:10; Php. 1:11)
[296] (Tt. 1:16)
[297] (Eph. 4:22-24)

Jesus, Who dwells in us[298]. We are now seated with Christ Jesus in Heaven, and therefore our lifestyle that we now have is in Heaven[299]. Now as the citizens of Heaven, we can be holy in every dimension of our behavior[300].

Godliness expresses a devotion to the ways of God. God has set apart the godly for Himself. In the Hebrew language, the word for godly is חָסִיד ('chasid'). In the Greek language, its equivalence is εὐσεβής ('eusebes'). Godliness is a devotion to the righteousness of God. When we were born again, God gave us His life and godliness, and we are called to grow and develop in both[301]. Paul sets godliness in a moral equivalence to righteousness when He tells us to deny all ungodliness and live righteously and godly in this present world[302]. Paul sets godliness and righteousness as that which we are to follow after, and as the chief characteristics of our lives in contrast to all the works of sin and iniquity[303].

Righteousness is forever and forever[304]. God in His great love and mercy gave us His righteousness. His righteousness is so perfect and so high above all things that no person could ever **earn** it, so He gave it to us to **learn** it. At the first moment of salvation, when we were

---

[298] (Php. 1:27)
[299] (Eph. 2:6; 3:20)
[300] (1 Pet. 1:15; Php. 3:20)
[301] (2 Pet. 1:3-10)
[302] (Tt. 2:12)
[303] (1 Tim. 6:11; Tt. 2:12)
[304] (Ps. 112:6; 119:142; Prov. 10:25)

Made Righteous by Faith

born again and created in Christ Jesus, we were made as righteous as He is righteous. We were born into righteousness and given the Spirit of righteousness to learn righteousness and have the fruits of righteousness. Now as His sons and daughters, as His priest and kings, we are being mentored by the Holy Spirit. In His great love and compassion for us, He develops us in the righteousness that we were given. He establishes us in His reign of righteousness to reign with Him now and forever[305].

All of God's judgments are righteous and God shall judge the world by His righteousness[306]. God, who is the righteous judge and the standard for all righteousness, is the One who examines the righteous[307]. It's His own righteousness that is acceptable to Him, and His righteousness has been given to everyone who has called on the name of Jesus. The everlasting righteousness that God has is the standard of His Kingdom and can only be received as a gift by the gift-giver, Christ Jesus. Without His righteousness, all are unrighteous, no matter how right they believe themselves to be. Now God commands all men everywhere to repent, because He has appointed a day, in which He will judge the world in righteousness by that Man Whom He has ordained – in Whom He has given assurance unto all men, in that He has raised Him

---
[305] (Rom. 5:17; Heb. 1:8; Isa. 32:17; 51:8; 60:21; 1 Jn. 3:7)
[306] (Ps. 9:8; 19:9)
[307] (Ps. 11:4)

from the dead[308]. All judgment is given to the Son, Christ Jesus but He judges no man. The Word which He has spoken shall judge each person[309]. In Him we have nothing to fear, because we have His righteousness and holiness. We are fully acceptable to God in Christ Jesus. We live and abide in His love.

> *"And we have known and believed the love that God has for us. God is love; and he that dwells in love dwells in God, and God in him. Herein is our love made perfect: that we may have boldness in the day of judgment, because as He is, so are we in this world."*
>
> (1 Jn. 4:16–17)

---

[308] (Ac. 17:30–31)
[309] (Jn. 5:22; 12:48)

The Fruits of Righteousness

"Being filled with the fruits of righteousness, which are by Jesus Christ, unto the glory and praise of God."
(Php. 1:11)

There is nothing that could speak more loudly to the truth that being made righteous will produce God's righteousness than having the fruits of righteousness. The righteousness which is by Christ Jesus has empowered us to live His life of righteousness. It's impossible to imagine a more wonderful life than living the one that God has designed. The life of righteousness is the way that God lives and what could be a greater honor and blessing than to live like God lives. Because of His presence in our lives, we become like a garden in which God brings forth all the fruits of His life – the fruits of righteousness. These fruits of righteousness are by Jesus Christ to the glory of God[310]. The rivers of God that flow out of us are described by the prophet Ezekiel as bringing forth life and fruitfulness

---

[310] (Php. 1:11)

everywhere they flow[311]. Christ Jesus described Himself as the vine and everyone who comes to Him as a branch. If we live in Him and rely solely upon Him we are able to bring forth the fruit of His life[312].

God has given us the ability to live a heavenly life now on this earth in an earthly body. He has adorned our bodies, which are His temples, with all the treasures and glory of the beauty of holiness. He has honored us with the highest of honors to be clothed in His righteousness[313]. To be taught in the ways of His majesty. To be entrusted with the honor of representing His ways to the nations. He has redeemed us and purified a people zealous of His good works[314]. These works are the expressions of His heavenly life. It's a life that we now live in the Holy Spirit. His life that is like a wellspring, springing up with all that only He can supply – His life that is like rivers, which flow out with goodness and righteousness and truth[315]. If we will only be willing every day we will find ourselves going from strength to strength and from glory to glory. We will increase more and more as we increase with the increase of God. This is the life that we will live throughout eternity in His presence. It's a life of heaven on earth[316].

---

[311] (Ezek. 47:1-12)
[312] (Jn. 15:1-7)
[313] (Isa. 61:10; Ps. 132:9)
[314] (Tt. 2:14)
[315] (Eph. 5:9-10)
[316] (Eph. 1:3; Col. 1:13; Deut. 11:21)

Made Righteous by Faith

The Lord Jesus tells us above all other things to seek the kingdom of God and His righteousness. One of the most important things about this is recognizing that the righteousness of the Kingdom of God comes to us by the Holy Spirit[317]. Knowing that the Holy Spirit's life flows out of us like rivers, we should have righteousness flowing out like rivers[318]. There are those who have mistakenly referred to these expressions of the Holy Spirit as self righteousness. Self righteousness is that which a person would do of their own ability to earn some favor or position with God. Self righteousness is most accurately described as Law-works to earn a status of righteousness. The righteousness that is by the Holy Spirit is divine righteousness and has absolutely nothing to do with self righteousness. It's the righteousness that comes by Jesus Christ, for without Him we can do nothing[319]. God trains us in His righteousness and teaches us how to yield to Him. The divine life provides the growth and development of life and godliness[320]. God's divine power at work in us provides excellence of character, faith, knowledge, self control, patience, godliness, brotherly kindness, and love[321]. All of the fruits of the Spirit can be understood as part of the righteousness of God that we have received,

---

[317] (Rom. 14:17; Lk. 12:32; Gal. 5:22-23)
[318] (Jn. 7:39)
[319] (Jn. 15:5)
[320] (2 Pet. 1:3; 3:18; 1 Pet. 2:2; Eph. 4:15)
[321] (2 Pet. 1:4-7)

not earned![322] Yet, still we grow and develop in the fruits of righteousness by the Holy Spirit Who produces them.

The reality is that there is going to be some kind of fruit in our lives. It will either be the fruits of righteousness or unrighteousness. As Paul said,

> "Don't you know, whomever you yield yourselves servants to obey, his servants you are to whomever you obey; whether of sin unto death, or of obedience unto righteousness."
>
> (Rom. 6:15–16)

There is no middle ground. God is patient and longsuffering to develop us. He provides His love, mercy and forgiveness for all who seek it as He trains us to walk in His ways. However, we should make no mistake, all the ways of God are in righteousness[323]. We cannot say that we are walking in the ways of God if we are not walking in His righteousness. The plea of God is that we awake unto righteousness and sin not[324].

If we are following after righteousness, then we are learning to give no place to sin. Simply, righteousness is doing that which is right in the eyes of the Lord and sin is doing those things that are evil in the eyes of the Lord. We are going to do one or the other! We will either have the fruits of righteousness or the fruits of unrighteousness. To

---
[322] (Gal. 5:22-23)
[323] (Ps. 145:17; Prov. 8:20, 12:28; 13:6; Ps. 85:13)
[324] (1 Cor. 15:24)

think that there is some kind of neutral ground where neither occurs is very naive. The instruction of the Holy Spirit to us is to "flee youthful lusts: but follow righteousness, faith, love, peace, with them that call on the Lord out of a pure heart"[325]. We cannot allow ourselves to be deceived by all the "rational" and "logical" thinking of men. John said in very plain and simple language, "Little children, let no man deceive you: he who does righteousness is righteous, even as He is righteous"[326]. Christ Jesus Who is our righteousness dwells in us. He dwells in us by the Spirit Who He has given us[327]. He is the One at work on the inside of us, bringing forth fruit unto God[328]. We are His – we belong to Him. We are not our own. If we are willing, then the life that we now live is His life, and God will manifest His Son in us[329].

O'Brien defines "righteousness" in Php. 1:11 as "ethical characteristics" that are evidence of a right relationship between a believer and God. He contends that this interpretation squares with the wider New Testament metaphorical use of 'karpos' to refer to "the result, outcome, or profit of an action" regarding the Christian life.[330][331]

---

[325] (2 Tim. 2:21–22; 1 Tim. 6:11)
[326] (1 Jn. 2:29; 3:7; 10)
[327] (1 Jn. 3:24)
[328] (Php. 2:13; Eph. 3:20; 2 Cor. 4:7)
[329] (Gal. 1:16; Col. 1:27; Gal 2:20; Php. 1:21)
[330] (see Mt. 3:8; 7:16; Rom. 1:13; 1 Cor. 9:7; Eph. 5:9; 2 Tim. 2:6)
[331] (O'Brien, Peter Thomas. 1991)

F.F. Bruce views the "fruit of righteousness" in Pp.l 1:11 as an identical way of referring to the "fruit of Spirit" (see Gal. 5:22–23). Believers bear this "fruit" as a result of the new life implanted in them. Their union with Christ through faith enables them to produce the "fruit of righteousness," which Christ Himself perfectly manifested[332]

Martin claims that the "fruit of righteousness" refers to the righteousness that believers receive through Christ (see Php. 3:9); on the other hand, it also refers to the evidence of having a right relationship with God (i.e., fruit that consists of being right with God).[333].

Melick says the fruit or righteousness refers not to "imputed righteousness," but to ethical righteousness. He finds support for this understanding in Old Testament passages such as Hos. 10:12. He says Christ produces this righteousness in believers as they live in an acceptable way to Him.[334]

Witherington, says Paul is concerned with imparted righteousness, not imputed righteousness. In other words, Paul is referring to "inward and moral righteousness" as the outworking of the believer's upright life. The bearing of this fruit, Witherington says, enables believers to be "blameless" and "pure" at the eschaton. In his view, "righteousness" in Php. 1:11 also has a forensic sense and

---

[332] (Bruce, F. F. 2011).
[333] (Martin, Ralph P. 1974)
[334] (Melick, Richard R. 1991)

relates to God's decree since the verse appears in an eschatological and forensic context.[335]

Osborne says that the fruit here would be linked with the fruit of the Spirit in Galatians 5:22–23 and the fruitful branches of John 15:1–8. "Righteousness" refers to the righteous work of God in our lives and our virtuous living that results.[336]

---

[335] (Witherington, Ben. 2011)
[336] (Osborne Grant R. , 2017)

Faith and Obedience

"If a man loves me, he will keep my words: and my Father will love him, and we will come unto him, and make our abode with him."

(Jn. 14:23)

The obedience of Christ Jesus is ours to have. The one who learned obedience by the things that He suffered has given us the same Spirit of holiness that He has[337]. The One who overcame has given us His overcoming power[338]. We have been given both His obedience and His overcoming power because He now dwells in us. We have His life therefore we have His righteousness and His holiness. His obedience came to us by His blood shed and His Spirit of obedience[339]. The power or the great exploits of the Spirit that were upon the men of old like Samson is now in our inner being. Through Adam's disobedience we were made sinners but through the obedience of Jesus we were made righteous[340]. The spirit of disobedience ruled

---

[337] (Heb. 5:8; Rom. 1:3)
[338] (Rev. 2:7; 1 Jn. 4:4)
[339] (1 Pet. 1:2)
[340] (Rom. 5:19)

us under the dominion of sin and death, but we have been born again! Now we are to allow the Spirit of obedience to rule. As the children of God, Christ Jesus is our King and should be allowed to reign supreme over our lives[341]. We have been given the divine ability to bring every thought into captivity unto His obedience, the obedience of Christ[342]. He is our Good Shepherd who laid His life down for us, and as the resurrected Shepherd He leads us[343]. Surely, God who spared not His own Son but delivered Him up for us all, shall also freely give us everything that we need to fulfill all that He desires[344].

God does not make works and obedience mutually exclusive. Once again these are faith-works, the fruits of righteousness. Works of obedience to God is a response to the loving relationship and union that we now have with Him. Our response is to follow the One who called us and ordained us to follow Him. Abraham had a relationship with God and out of that relationship he obeyed God. Some of the greatest examples of obedience in all the Old Testament were demonstrated by Abraham. Abraham's willingness to follow God, trust God, and obey God, even to the sacrificing of Isaac, was the greatest example of what God the Father of our Lord Jesus Christ did for us.

---

[341] (Eph. 2:2)
[342] (2 Cor. 10:4)
[343] (Jn. 10:27; 1 Pet. 2:25)
[344] (Rom. 8:32)

In contrast to Abraham's obedience to God is the disobedience of His descendants, Israel. God gives us an overview of their response to Him in Hebrews 3:7-4:11. God shows us a correlation between their disobedience and unbelief, a pattern which follows that of obedience to faith. The children of Israel refused to learn the ways of God and as a result had hardened their hearts through unbelief. One of the deadly results of sin is that it causes a hardening of the heart. The continual disobedience of sin is born out of unbelief and it can only have one result: the hardening of the heart[345]. Their unbelief was the cause of their sin and because of it they could not enter into the promises of God. Because of their unwillingness to obey God, the Lord did not give them eyes to see, or ears to hear, or hearts to understand[346]. Ultimately because they continued to harden their hearts in disobedience He took the opportunity away altogether[347].

> *"And he said, Go, and tell this people Hear indeed, but understand not; And see indeed, but perceive not. Make the heart of these people fat, And make their ears heavy, and shut their eyes, Lest they see with their eyes, and hear with their ears, And understand with their heart, and convert, and be healed."*
>
> (Isa. 6:9-10)

---

[345] (Heb. 3:10-13, 17-19)
[346] (Dt. 29:4)
[347] Mt. 13:14; Jn. 12:40; Ac. 28:26)

The gospel was preached to them, but they refused to allow the gospel to be mixed with faith[348]. They refused to hear and obey – instead, disobedience was their ruin. He spoke to them with an audible voice. He performed great wonders and miracles among them. Yet still they refused to hear His voice and obey His instruction. We must take heed and recognize that we also run the same risk. If we refuse to hear His voice, who is now speaking from heaven, our end will be worse[349]. If we refuse to obey those things that He has asked of us, then we will fall into the same snare that they fell into. Their unbelief was expressed in their disobedience and their disobedience plunged them into greater unbelief. The first lesson of Scripture is that disobedience results in sin and death[350].

Obedience to God by the Spirit of obedience is very different from Law-works. There are different kinds of works referred to in the Bible:

- Law-works, (ritual and tradition)[351]
- Dead works (works that lead to death)[352]
- Works of the flesh (the unregenerate state)[353]

---

[348] (Heb. 4:2, 6)
[349] (Heb. 12:25)
[350] (Rom. 5:19; 6:16-23; Jas. 1:13-15)
[351] Rom. 3:20; 9:32; 10:3; Gal. 2:11-13, 16; 3:2, 10; Lk. 18:12; Mt. 23:25; etc.
[352] Heb 6:1; 9:14; Rom. 13:14
[353] Rom. 7:5; 8:1-9; Gal. 5:19-21; 1 Jn. 3:8, 19; etc.

- Works of the Spirit (faith works/regenerated life)[354]
- Self-works (human ability)[355]

In the Western World, Law-works are rare, especially among Christians. Once again, when James speaks of works, he is referring to the works of the Spirit. Why? Because he is speaking about what comes forth from faith. The life of the born again believer should be the works of the Holy Spirit. Certainly not of the futile works of the flesh (unregenerate state) or of human ability. We are to be those who walk not after the flesh but after the Spirit. We have been empowered by God to live in the Spirit.

When James refers to faith he is speaking of the whole of the life of the born again believer. He puts forth the simplest argument possible to help everyone understand that faith in Christ Jesus is a lifestyle. Therefore faith without works does not exist. Abraham was shown to be righteous by works. What was he doing? He was obeying God in the most extreme way and the promise of the Seed was once again confirmed to Him because of his obedience[356]. He was taking his son Isaac, in obedience to

---

[354] Gal. 5:22-23; Jas. 2:20; Rom. 8:13; 15:18; Ac. 26:20; Rom. 2:15, 13:12; 1 Cor. 3:13-14, 15:58, 16:10; 2 Cor. 9:8, 11:15; Gal. 6:4; Eph. 2:10; Php. 2:12, 30; Col. 1:10, 29; 1 Thess. 1:3, 5:13; 2 Thess. 2:17; 1 Tim. 2:10, 5:10, 25, 6:18; 2 Tim. 2:21, 3:17; Tt. 1:16, 2:7, 14, 3:1, 8, 14; Heb. 6:10, 10:24, 13:21 etc.
[355] Gal. 3:3; 4:23; Jn. 5:30; 8:28; 12:39; 14:10; Mt. 26:41; 2 Cor 1:12; 2 Cor 10:2 etc.
[356] (Gen. 22:17)

God, and offering him as a human sacrifice to God[357]. The righteousness of faith was counted unto him but still, there was a continual ongoing expression of his relationship with God. His relationship with God was expressed by His obedience. Abraham did not earn a relationship with God; he was invited into the relationship. We do not earn a relationship with God. We do not earn righteousness; it was all given to us. Still, if we love Him we will obey His word[358]. Obedience is not a violation of faith- its the expression of faith. Even the love that Jesus had for the Father was expressed by obedience[359]. We began the relationship by obeying God. We repent and call upon the name of the Lord Jesus for salvation. The relationship then continues in obedience as we walk out this love relationship by the Spirit[360]. The love of God poured into our heart by the Holy Spirit causes us to dwell in His love. The love is pure and holy and produces all the fruits of righteousness which are by Christ Jesus.

---

[357] (Gen. 22:1-19)
[358] (Jn. 14:15, 21, 23)
[359] (Jn. 14:31; Heb. 5:8)
[360] (1 Pet. 1:14, 22; 1 Jn. 3:22-24)

Law Righteousness

"according to zeal, persecuting the church, concerning the righteousness which is in the Law, blameless."
(Php. 3:6)

God did not give the Law to Moses as a means to attain righteousness. Certainly, obedience to the Law of God was considered acts of righteousness, but not God's righteousness[361]. Paul said, concerning the righteousness that was by the Law, he was blameless[362]. Similar to the rich young man who had kept all of the commandments, there was the ability even in unredeemed men to obey God[363]. Still, it was never the purpose of the Law to make one righteous. Paul recognized that even though he was blameless with regards to keeping the Law, still He knew that true righteousness, the righteousness of God, could not come by the Law[364]. The Law was added to the promise because of transgression against the promise[365].

---

[361] (Dt. 6:25)
[362] (Php. 3:6)
[363] (Mk. 10:20-21)
[364] (Gal. 2:21; Rom. 3:22-25; 10:3)
[365] (Gal. 3:19)

The promise was all about the coming Seed[366]. The purpose of the Law was to serve as the means by which the Children of Israel would be set apart unto God and separated from the idolatry of the nations around them. It would be a schoolmaster to bring them to Christ[367].

Even though Israel followed the Law, they did not attain the righteousness of the Law – they never approached it as Abraham did[368]. They always saw it as a means to an end in itself and refused to see that it would be abolished as the means to approach God when the Seed would come[369]. However, even though Israel missed the point altogether, there was a remnant of the people who, like Abraham, would walk with God and believe in the coming Seed. Through the remnant God would bring forth the Seed, the Redeemer, Christ Jesus. Through the Law, God raised up a young girl who was highly favored – a young virgin named Mary – from this remnant. He raised up a righteous man like Joseph to be her husband[370]. He had a righteous man like Simeon to witness His arrival[371]. He had two righteous servants like Zacharias and Elizabeth to bring forth His prophet (Lk. 1:6). Their righteousness was not because they kept the Law but, like Abraham, and all the other righteous that are

---

[366] (Gal. 3:16)
[367] (Gal. 3:24; 4:2)
[368] (Rom. 9:31)
[369] (2 Cor. 3:13)
[370] (Mt. 1:19)
[371] (Lk. 2:25)

named in the Old Testament, they had faith in the coming Seed, Christ Jesus. Still they were in need of the righteousness of God that only the New Birth could bring.

God set apart the family of Abraham for Himself. He made a promise to Abraham that the One Who would redeem us and restore our union with God would come from his Seed. The promise would come in the fullness of time and provide God's redemption for all humanity. The Eternal Word would be made flesh and born of a virgin who was a descendant of Abraham. Abraham's children would suffer many things between the promise and the birth of the Messiah. Many of those things that they suffered was because of their rejections of God's commands. God gave them His Law of commandments to guide them and keep them separate from all the demonic practices of the world around them, but they failed to listen. He gave them the Law and commandments of His ways so that He might dwell among them. He gave them His Laws so that they might know their need for the Redeemer[372].

The Law would be as a schoolmaster to bring them to the redemption that God would offer by His Own Son. The Law was not evil – it was just, good, and holy because it was from God. It was the means by which He made the

---

[372] (Gal. 3:24)

Made Righteous by Faith

people holy and set them apart unto Himself[373]. Moses told the people,

> *"And it shall be our righteousness, if we observe to do all these commandments before the LORD our God, as he has commanded."*
>
> (Dt. 6:25)

This was God's plan, not man's. Although the Law was powerless to impart the life of God it would serve to instruct them and bring them to a better hope[374]. Paul said the Law is "holy, righteous, and good," and "spiritual" (Rom. 7:12). We can even understand the instruction from the scriptures as "God-breathed"[375]. However, by the time Jesus the Messiah came the Jews had turned the Law into a system of self-righteousness. Their traditions had so taken over that Jesus told them that they had rejected the commandments of God in order to keep their traditions[376]. Their rules and regulations had so led them away from God they could not recognize the Messiah. Their whole concepts of righteousness and keeping the law had become completely distorted[377]. Their traditions of self righteousness had blinded them so that they could

---

[373] (Ex. 19:6; Lev. 19:2; Dt. 19:7)
[374] (Gal. 3:21; Heb. 7:19)
[375] (2 Tim. 3:16)
[376] (Mk. 7:9, 13; Mt. 15:3, 6)
[377] (John Lightfoot, 1663)

not recognize the voice of God, nor their Redeemer. They had lost all sight of their need for redemption.

After the return of the people of Israel from Babylon they begin to formulate their own religious system based on the Law. These traditions would establish a method of how to earn righteousness with God[378]. Once a certain level of righteousness was attained they could claim a special union with God and a special access to Him. This was what Paul referred to as "going about to establish their own righteousness."[379] Their interactions with Jesus highlights some of the more important rules that they had made in their legalistic system to obtain righteousness. They had so distorted the Law that it had become a legal system by which they could obtain salvation. In their minds they did not need a savior, the Law was their savior.[380]

> "They had become so deceived by their legal system that they believed their righteousness in the Law was all they needed to deal with sin but for the purification of the body; supposing still that the soul was thoroughly purified beforehand by righteousness."
>
> (Flavius Josephus and William Whiston, 1987)

---

[378] (Ronald L. Eisenberg, 2004; Michael L. Rodkinson, 1918)
[379] (Rom. 10:3)
[380] (Jn. 8:31-41, 9:34)

They boasted of being the children of Abraham and being keepers of the Law, and so to them a Redeemer was not needed. Rather, they looked for the Messiah Who would come and be King. Their self-righteousness, which was their vain attempts to be made righteous before God, was actually unrighteousness.

There are many examples of the rituals and traditions that they had derived from the Law which they believed made them righteous[381]. In fact, they believed that the more they did them, the more righteous they became. One of the many examples of their disposition about their own righteousness is found in the example Jesus gave of a Pharisee in contrast to a tax collector. The Pharisee trusting in his own righteousness prayed,

> "God, I thank You, that I am not as other men are: extortioners, unrighteous, adulterers, or even as this publican."
>
> (Lk. 18:11)

Their view of themselves was that through their observance of their traditions they were not sinners but righteous[382].

One of the many traditions that they believed made them righteous was the giving of alms. They thought that the more alms they gave to the poor, the more righteous

---

[381] (See Jacob Neusner, 2008)
[382] (Mt. 5:20; Lk. 20:46)

they were. Giving alms was good and encouraged by Jesus, but not to earn righteousness. It should have rather simply been about having compassion on the poor. He exposed their hypocrisy in self-righteousness in their giving to God when He said,

> *"for you pay tithe of mint and anise and cummin, and have omitted the weightier matters of the Law: judgment, mercy, and faith: these you should have done, and not to left the other undone."*
>
> (Mt. 23:23)

They thought that their strict rules of washing before eating, regarding the sabbath day, fasting twice a week, the wearing of phylacteries and many other misplaced ideas earned them righteousness. Keep in mind they were not interested in learning righteousness – they were wanting to earn righteousness to gain a higher standing among the community of Israel. Jesus shows the misplaced ideas that they had about the Law of Moses and the legalism that bound them when He ate with sinners[383]. Their self righteous superiority was exemplified at Simon the leper's house when they disqualified Jesus because He let a woman who was a sinner touch Him[384].

The Mishnah – which codified these Jewish traditions for obtaining righteousness – was written out in the

---
[383] (Mk. 2:16; Lk. 5:30)
[384] (Lk. 7:37, 39)

second century A.D. In reading the Mishnah and its commentary, the Talmud, we come to understand how far their traditions became removed from the Law of Moses[385]. This is why Jesus said,

> *"Woe unto you, lawyers! For you have taken away the key of knowledge: you entered not in yourselves, and they who were entering in you hindered."*
>
> (Lk. 11:52)

Jesus also said regarding their traditions that by keeping their traditions they made the commandments of God meaningless[386]. It was this Jewish religious system that defined what legalism was. Works based salvation can't be more perfectly described – than this religious system that was strictly followed in order to earn righteousness and gain God's blessing.

> "Some consideration of Jewish teaching is necessary, if we would rightly appreciate the teaching of the New Testament on the subject. Evidence of the importance which had been acquired for religious minds among the Jews of the 2nd or 3rd century B.C. has already come before us in the fact that a special name was assigned to this class of actions. They had become one of the common and acknowledged observances of the religious life, a

---
[385] (Jacob Neusner, 1988).
[386] (Mk. 7:9; Mt 15:3, 6)

matter to be attended to by the religious man in the same regular and careful manner as prayer and fasting, with which we find these joined (see Tobit 12:8, Sirach 7:10, and cf. the conduct of the earnest proselyte Cornelius, Ac. 10:2, 4). It is regarded as a specially efficacious means of making atonement for sin (Sirach 3:14, 30; 16:14), and obtaining divine protection from calamity (Sirach 29:12; 40:24; Tobit 14:10-11); the merit thereof is an unfailing possession (Sirach 40:17); the religious reputation to be won thereby is held out as an inducement to the practice of it (Sirach 31 [LXX 34]:11). Such features in the estimate of these are, if possible, still more marked in the Talmud, where צְדָקָה ('sedaqah,' "righteousness") is a recognised name for the religious. <u>The performance of works of mercy is set forth as a means whereby man may be accounted righteous in the sight of God</u>, like the fulfilment of the commandments of the Law. It is even more meritorious than the latter, because it is not exactly prescribed, but left, as to its extent and amount at least, to the individual."

(F. Weber, 1880)

These among even the more legitimate Law-works like circumcision, dietary rules, and sabbath-keeping were the works that Paul was opposed to if they in any way identified their salvation with them. These are the works that the Jews did in an attempt to establish their own righteousness[387].

---

[387] (Rom. 10:3)

Those Who Were Righteous in the Old Testament

"And the LORD said unto Noah, Come you and all your house into the ark; for you have I seen righteous before me in this generation."

(Gen. 7:1)

In Romans, Paul describes the whole world in sin. He quotes the words of the Psalmist saying, "there is none righteous, no not one"[388].

"There is none that understands; there is none that seeks after God. They are all gone out of the way, they are together become unprofitable; there is none who does good – no, not one. Their throat is an open sepulcher; with their tongues they have used deceit; the poison of asps is under their lips; whose mouth is full of cursing and bitterness. Their feet are swift to

---

[388] (Ps. 14:1-3; 53:1-3)

Made Righteous by Faith

shed blood. Destruction and misery are in their ways, and the way of peace they have not known: There is no fear of God before their eyes. Now we know that what the Law says, it says to those who are under the Law, that every mouth may be stopped, **and all the world may become guilty before God.** *Therefore by the deeds of the Law there shall no flesh be made righteous in his sight: for by the Law is the knowledge of sin."*

(Rom. 3:11–20)

Once again there was no law that was ever given that would make a person righteous. **The Law was given to make the whole world guilty before God.** Paul showed that the Law of God proved that the whole world was in need of a Savior. Especially the Jews that refused to acknowledge their need for one and trusted in the Law for salvation. That had lost sight of the promise and faith in the coming Seed. It was Paul's desire to convince those who believed themselves to be righteous that in fact they were unrighteous[389]. Those who thought they could be made righteous by the Law gained much of Paul's attention in Romans chapters 3-4 and Galatians chapters 2-3. It was Paul's earnest desire to convince his Jewish brethren that they were all in need of a Savior[390].

---

[389] (Rom. 9:1-5, 31; 10:1-3; Gal. 1:14)
[390] (Rom. 9:3-4; 10:1-2)

Still, there were those that God identified in the Bible as righteous. There were those who followed in the faith of Abraham and looked for the coming Redeemer which God had testified to throughout their generations[391]. Just as God had made Israel a holy people through the covenant of the Law he also gave those who walked with Him in faith the same righteousness by faith that He had given to Abraham. The same opportunity to be the righteous who lived by faith that Habakkuk referred to[392]. This was a relationship that was also witnessed by Balaam when he spoke by the Spirit of the Lord and said,

"who can count the dust of Jacob and the number of the fourth part of Israel? Let me die the death of the righteous and let my last end be as his,"

"He has not beheld iniquity in Jacob, Neither has he seen perverseness in Israel."

(Num. 23:10, 21)

There were many that God called righteous both before and after the Law of Moses was given. Some of those that were called righteous were: Noah, Daniel, Job, Lot, and Abraham[393]. We certainly are able to understand the qualification of righteousness through the life of Abraham. Abraham was righteous because He believed

---

[391] (Lk. 1:67-73; Rom. 1:25; 1 Pet. 1:12; Hab. 2:4; Heb. 11:39)
[392] (Hab. 2:4; Heb. 1:1-39)
[393] (Gen. 7:1; Job 1:1; Gen. 15:6; Ezek. 14:14, 20; 2 Pet. 2:8)

Made Righteous by Faith

the Word of God, and more specifically he believed in the Seed, the coming Redeemer. It is certainly safe to say that everyone else that was considered righteous and had a relationship with God before Christ Jesus had faith in the One who was to come. God said concerning Noah, Daniel, and Job, that in the context of the wickedness of Israel that they only would be able to deliver their own souls by their righteousness[394].

We know that God led the covenant children of Israel in the paths of righteousness but few seemed willing to be led[395]. We also know that the path led to Jesus Christ the Redeemer. God had many things to say about the righteous, what they were like and how to walk in righteousness[396]. There were those who had faith to do righteousness before Christ Jesus came[397]. Certainly that faith was faith in the coming Redeemer[398]. The cry of God to the people of Israel to do righteousness was heard many times. God said, "But let judgment run down as waters, And righteousness as a mighty stream."[399] The righteousness in conduct that God desired then was the same that He desires now – to believe what God had spoken and be obedient to His word[400].

---

[394] (Ezek. 14:20)
[395] (Ps. 23:3)
[396] (Ps. 11:5; Prov. 10:3; 11:30; 13:25; Ezek. 3:21; 14:4)
[397] (Heb. 11:1-39)
[398] (Heb. 11:33, 39-40; 1 Pet 1:12; Hab. 2:4)
[399] (Am. 5:24)
[400] (1 Sam. 15:22; Isa. 1:19; Hab. 2:4; Rom. 15:18; 1 Pet. 1:2, 14; 2 Cor. 10:5-6)

The Lord addressed those who were righteous many times in the Old Testament. He referred to the righteous about 411 times. God made many promises concerning righteousness in the Old Testament. The righteous were identified as those who obeyed God and kept His word. They were the undefiled who walked in the Law of the Lord and were those who did no iniquity but walked in His ways[401]. David said concerning the righteous that he had never seen them forsaken or their children begging for bread[402]. God promised that His eyes would be upon the righteous and that His ears would be opened to their prayers. Once again they were qualified as those who depart from evil[403]. Although there were many afflictions that were suffered by the righteous, the LORD delivered them from them all[404]. It was only those who were righteous that God would have a relationship with. God promised to bless the righteous and lead the righteous in the paths of righteousness[405]. He made known to them that it would be those who walk uprightly and worked righteousness that would dwell in His holy mountain[406]. He rewarded His servants according to their righteousness. It was the righteous who were glad and the

---

[401] (Ps. 119:1-3)
[402] (Ps. 37:25)
[403] (Ps. 34:13-17)
[404] (Ps. 34:19)
[405] (Ps. 1:6; 5:12; 22:3; 85:13; 97:12; 106:3; 140:13; Prov. 2:9, 20; 8:20; 11:5; 12:26, 28; 15:9, 19; 16:31)
[406] (Ps. 15:1-5; 24:3-6)

upright who shouted for joy[407]. The righteous in the Old Testament were all those who knew God and obeyed Him.

---

[407] (Ps. 32:11; 132:9)

The Righteousness of Faith Speaks

"But the righteousness which is of faith speaks like this..."

(Rom. 10:6)

The righteousness of faith says this: Christ Jesus is here, and His word of faith is in my mouth – the Word of God that is spirit and life; the Word of God that is powerful; the Word of God that framed the universe. He has put His Word in our hearts and mouths – His Word of faith! The Word of faith testifies that we have believed with our heart unto righteousness. We have called on the name of the Lord Jesus and our confession is that we are saved. We are saved because God, who is faithful and cannot lie, says we are saved. This is one of the many messages that the Apostle Paul taught directly from the books of the Law. It is a direct quote from Deuteronomy 30:12-14. In Deuteronomy, Moses was pleading with the people to love God with all of their heart and soul. His plea was not about a legislative religious system, but the desire of God to have a love relationship with them. This is not a relationship initiated by man, but by God. It is not an attempt to earn a relationship, but to respond to an invitation directly from God to enter into His family. All that God had purposed man to become, all that He desired man to be was now found in Christ Jesus His Only Begotten Son. When Christ Jesus came and brought the transformation of life and nature, all that God had promised was fulfilled. He established His ways in our hearts and minds and the intimate union of love was born[408]. Salvation begins in the inward parts through which God gives us His resurrected life and righteousness[409]. The Holy Spirit trains us and mentors us in all that God has done for us which we observe as the fruits of salvation, the fruits of righteousness. The evidence of being made right.

The salvation that we have received is more than position or standing with God because it is a definite change of heart and life. We not only find ourselves in Christ Jesus, He is also found in us. There are several summary salvation scriptures in the New Testament that both define salvation and give the breadth of its impact[410]. If we just consider the Greek word for New Testament salvation it is insightful, liberating, and empowering. The Greek word for salvation is σῴζω ('sozo'). It can be

---
[408] (Heb. 8:10, 10:16; Eph. 5:30; Jn. 6:56; 17:21-23)
[409] (Col. 2:12; 3:1-3; 1 Pet. 1:3)
[410] (Tt. 3:5; 2 Cor. 5:17-18; 1 Cor. 1:30; 6:11; and Rom. 8:1)

translated by several words, but the most common as well as meaningful is to "save" or "deliver." We understand this word by many examples in the Old Testament. God saved Noah and His family[411]. God saved Lot and his wife and two daughters from Sodom and Gomorrah[412]. He delivered Israel from the tyranny of Pharaoh and their slavery in Egypt. God raised up deliverers in the book of Judges to rescue the repentant Israelites from their captivity. There is no concept of salvation or deliverance that left those who were saved in some kind of "positional salvation."

The Greek word 'sozo' covers a broad spectrum of deliverance. It includes the physical, spiritual, and financial dimensions of our lives. It's the salvation that only God can bring to pass, a salvation that is the revelation of His own power and divine ability. The salvation that completely saves.

Various definitions:
- To "preserve" or "rescue" from natural dangers and afflictions; "save," "keep from harm," "preserve," "rescue"[413]
- to "make safe," "make sound,"
    1. "to deliver from a direct threat"

---

[411] (Heb. 11:7)
[412] (Gen. 19:22)
[413] (BDAG, 2000)

2. "to bring safe and sound out of a difficult situation."[414]
- To "save," "deliver," "make whole," "preserve safe from danger, loss, or destruction"[415]

Being saved clearly means that we have been rescued from the power of sin and death. Satan has no more power over us than Pharaoh had over Israel after Passover. Sin has no more power over us to work in our lives than the taskmasters of Egypt had once the Israelites passed through the Red Sea. The righteousness of faith says that who the Son sets free is free indeed! The righteousness of faith speaks with the confession of who Christ Jesus is and what He has done for us. The righteousness of faith speaks and declares the deliverance and freedom that we now have in Christ Jesus. The righteousness of faith proclaims the gospel of redemption and union with Christ Jesus through New Birth. We are made righteous through the new creation. We are righteous because Christ Jesus dwells in us. Righteous because the very Spirit of righteousness dwells in us. Christ Jesus is our righteousness and He is in us and we are in Him[416]. We live out His life of righteousness under the ministry of righteousness.

---

[414] (Werner Foerster, 1964)
[415] (Spiros Zodhiates, 2000)
[416] (Jn. 6:56; 14:20-21, 23; 15:1-7; 17:21-23; 1 Jn. 3:24; 4:12-13, 15 etc)

The righteousness which came to us by the faith of Jesus Christ speaks and says: human effort cannot produce the incarnation (to bring Him down). Human effort and Law works cannot raise Him from the dead (to bring Him up). We do not have to cross the sea or search endlessly to discover it. It is too high and beyond the reach of all exploration and investigation of men. God – by His own power, in His great love – brought to pass every dimension of our salvation. God did not give Israel the land of promise because they were righteous[417]. He did not give us His life and righteousness by any works of righteousness which we might have done[418]. All that men could ever do could never attain the righteousness of God. God simply said, "Call and I will answer." We can even say that He put His words in our mouth so that we might know how to call and how to answer. He even answered before we called[419]. He has won our salvation by His own right arm. He keeps us by His own power. He perfects everything that concerns us and leads us in the way we should go. All we have to do is follow. We have confessed with our mouths and believed in our hearts unto righteousness. The righteousness that was purchased for us when Christ Jesus bore our sins away on the cross. The righteousness that was brought to us by the resurrection of Jesus from the dead. The righteousness that was given to

---
[417] (Dt. 9:4)
[418] (Tt. 3:15)
[419] (Isa. 65:24)

us when we were born again. The righteousness that came when old things passed away and everything became new.

What we must also realize in this realm of faith is that we now fulfill the righteousness of the Law because we have been born again and walk after the Spirit[420]. The love that only God possesses is now our possession too. His love was poured into our hearts by the Holy Spirit. His love now pours out of us by the Holy Spirit. It is the love that fulfills all of the Law and the Prophets[421]. We are no longer bound by sin and death[422]. We are no longer those who rely on human ability in an unregenerate state to walk in the ways of God. We have been born of the Spirit and now we walk in the Spirit[423]. We both live and walk in the divine life of Jesus provided for us by the Holy Spirit[424]. Therefore all those things that the Law testified to concerning the ways of God we are empowered by the Spirit of the Lord to do. All that belongs to the nature of God is at work within us by the Spirit which He has given us. The power of the divine nature, the power of the righteousness of God, the power of the holiness of God all at work within us. If we lack these things Peter said that we are blind and can't see far away and have forgotten that we were purged from our old sins[425]. Some may say what

---

[420] (Rom. 8:4)
[421] (Rom. 13:8, 10; Gal. 5:14; Jn. 13:34)
[422] (Rom. 8:3)
[423] (Rom. 8:1-9)
[424] (Gal. 5:16, 25)
[425] (2 Pet. 1:9)

things? The things supplied to us by the divine nature, the Spirit of the Lord[426]. That which God has given to us by His divine power[427]. Everything that pertains to His life and godliness so that we might walk in His glory and excellent character. This is what God has done for us. This is the work of faith that we embrace, a life of the Spirit and the ability that the Holy Spirit gives and not that of man.

> *"For the Law was powerless in that it was weak through the flesh. God sent His Son in the likeness of sinful flesh and concerning sin condemned sin in the flesh, that the righteousness of the Law might be fulfilled in us who walk not after the flesh but after the Spirit."*
>
> (Rom. 8:3-4)

---

[426] (2 Pet. 1:4)
[427] (2 Pet. 1:3)

Pleasing in His Sight

"And whatsoever we ask, we receive from Him, because we keep His commandments, and do those things that are pleasing in His sight."

(1 Jn. 3:22)

It's impossible to earn something with God. The idea of earning anything with God does not exist anywhere in the Bible. God is Holy beyond any holiness that could ever be earned. His righteousness is shown by the perfect and sinless life of Jesus. His righteousness and holiness can only be received as a gift, kept and established by the working of His mighty power, that will present us faultless on that day. It is this perfect righteousness and holiness that He gives us for the asking. It is His perfect righteousness that is credited to us. It is His life that is imparted to us so that we may say that we have the righteousness of God. Now in having received this unspeakable gift God teaches us to walk out His life.

Paul rebuked the false religious sect of the Jews in His day who thought that they could be pleasing to God by their own human efforts alone. They thought that their traditions would please God and earn them a position with God. They thought they could be made righteous on their own by the religious works developed out of their own traditions. They thought that through their works they could atone for their sins.

Those who Paul addressed who thought they could be right with God by their self-righteousness were very different from those like Zacharias and Elizabeth who God called "righteous"[428]. There were always those who looked for redemption among the people of Israel like Simeon[429]. Still today, something very different exists in our relationship with God through Christ Jesus. All of the sins of our past have been removed, wiped away by the blood of Jesus. We have a new heart and a new spirit, which was described by the prophets of old as the sign of the New Covenant[430]. It is only the new creation that pleases God[431]. It is by this alone that we are made acceptable to God. We have been given the Holy Spirit in a way that no one had in the past so that we might grow and develop in the ways of God[432]. We have been given the Spirit of the Son, and it should be our great desire to do the will of the Father and be pleasing in His sight[433]. The desire to walk pleasingly before the Lord has nothing to

---

[428] (Lk. 1:6)
[429] (Luke 2:25)
[430] (Jer. 31:33; Ezek. 11:19; 18:31; 36:26-27; Heb. 8:10; 10:16)
[431] (Gal. 5:16; 2 Cor. 5;17)
[432] (Jn. 7:39; Ac. 2:33)
[433] (Gal. 4:6, cr. 1:6)

Made Righteous by Faith

do with any concept of earning something with God – rather, it's walking out a love relationship that we have been given. We have been given the Holy Spirit as our Teacher and Guide Who leads us into all that pleases God. Doing what is right before God is not some form of self-righteousness – it's the righteousness that is by the faith of Jesus Christ at work in us.

There was absolutely nothing about the life of Jesus that was legalistic. He certainly honored the Scripture, which at that time was only the Old Testament. He honored everything that His heavenly Father requested to be done in the Law and went so far as to say that He did not come to destroy the Law, but to fulfill it[434]. Everything that Jesus did was about pleasing the Father[435]. We are called to follow the Lord Jesus in every way. God predestined us to be conformed to the image of the Son[436]. We have put on the Lord Jesus Christ and this new life that we are living is the life of Christ Jesus[437]. It should be our passionate desire to do the will of the Father. We have been honored with the ability to walk out a love relationship with God. The New Covenant instruction by the Apostles is that we walk pleasingly in every way and

---

[434] (Mt. 5:17-19)
[435] (Mk. 1:11; Jn. 8:29)
[436] (Rom. 8:29)
[437] (Rom. 13:14; 2 Cor. 5:17; Col. 1:27; 3:3; 1 Jn. 5:11; Php. 1:21; Gal. 2:20)

be fruitful in every good work[438]. We are to walk as Jesus walked, because as He is, so are we in this world[439].

Our lives are not supposed to be about pleasing men or even ourselves, but instead pleasing God[440]. The first commandment with promise that Paul called our attention to was not out of the New Testament – it was from the Old Testament, which was the Scripture that the Apostle Paul read before the audience that he ministered to. Paul was not forsaking those things that Father desired for all men to do[441]. Paul is not referring to Law-works or self-righteousness, which is a reference to men attempting to earn something with God. Rather, he is simply referring to the ability to live out the Word of God that has been written in our hearts and minds by the new birth. We now have the divine ability to be pleasing to God by doing the things that Father has asked us to do[442]. It's impossible to please God unless you have been born of the Spirit[443]. Being born of the Spirit and walking in the Spirit will be expressed in love actions as we honor that which our heavenly Father has asked of us. We have been instructed from both Testaments, especially the New Testament, how we are to walk and please God[444]. Paul said,

---

[438] (Col. 1:10)
[439] (1 Jn. 2:6; 4:17)
[440] (Gal. 1:10; Col. 3:20)
[441] (Eph. 6:2; Col. 3:20)
[442] (Rom. 3:31, 13:10; Jn. 14:21-23)
[443] (Rom. 8:8-9)
[444] (2 Tim. 2:4).

"that as you have received from us how you should walk and to please God, you should abound more and more."

(1 Thess. 4:1)

Enoch walked with God and pleased Him. The response that God had to Enoch was a great reward. It is in the context of the walk that Enoch had with God that we are told that without faith it is impossible to please God. Walking with God is a faith-walk, and the walk of faith is walking in the Spirit[445]. The Apostle John describes our walk of obedience to God's commands as our confidence that He hears us because we do what is pleasing in His sight[446]. Once again, this is not a vain attempt to earn anything with God. Rather, it's walking out the abundant life that we have received in Christ Jesus. It's a fellowship of love – and love desires to please.

Our Father in Heaven paid a high price for each one of us to enjoy the riches of His life. He gave us His very best. His only begotten Son to redeem us and His Holy Spirit to lead us. He teaches us the greatest things in life: how to love God and how to love each other. We learn how to live in His peace, His joy, and every dimension of His goodness. He teaches us how to live like the eternal God lives. He teaches us the ways of every good and perfect thing that comes from the Father of lights. He makes us

---
[445] (Heb. 11:5-6; Rom 8:8-9)
[446] (1 Jn. 3:22-24)

perfect in every good work to do His will[447]. He shows us how to let Him do through our lives what only He can do. In this walk of faith we find ourselves filled with His love and compassion for the world. We discover that nothing compares to His love and just how effortlessly His presence will flow from our lives like a mighty stream.

---

[447] (Jas. 1:17; Heb. 13:21)

Conclusion

"And if the righteous are barely saved, where will the ungodly and sinners appear?"

(1 Pet. 4:18)

There are two categories of people: those who are righteous and those who are ungodly and sinners. Clearly, the ungodly and sinners are in the category of the unrighteous. Both Peter and Jude cried out with the same message making known that God is no respecter of persons. His judgements concerning ungodliness and sin are the same now as in the past and will be the same forevermore. God judged the angels that sinned. He destroyed those in the days of Noah who sinned. He overthrew the cities of Sodom and Gomorrah because of their sin. He judged His people in the wilderness and those who rebelled died without mercy because of their sin. Paul said of how much worse punishment should we be thought worthy of if we trample under foot the blood of Jesus; if we reject His word and rulership over our lives. We cannot deny the Lordship, which is to say the rulership, of Jesus and believe that we are right with God.

We can't just say that Jesus Christ is our Savior if He is not also our Lord. Both Peter and Jude warned of the day that many would go astray and refuse the Lordship of Jesus, denying the One who purchased them. We cannot continue in sin and thank that we are living in the grace of God. God repeats the theme of the destructiveness of sin more than anything else in the Bible. He has shown His unwavering righteous judgments against all disobedience and ungodliness. Jesus made it very clear that His Word would judge us on the last day, so there will be no surprises. Today we are fast approaching the day of the great apostasy. The time when those who identify themselves as the people of God refuse conviction and correction. Many refuse the conviction and correction that comes from the Word of God and continue to justify themselves rather than be ruled by the Word of God and the Spirit of God. Many have eyes full of adultery and cannot cease from sin[448].

We are not to live by the subjective reasoning of men as to what is right or wrong. We are not to determine what is good or evil based on human conscience or cultural opinions. We are to live our lives by the Word of God. The Word of God and the Spirit of God guide us and reveal to us all that is right and pleasing to God. God has given us the power of the Name of Jesus, the blood of Jesus, and the authority of Jesus. We have been given the whole armor of

---

[448] (2 Pet. 2:14)

God. He has girded us with truth in the inwards parts and supplied us with His Own strength and with the power of His might. We are well equipped to resist the devil and stand against all of his deception. We have been given all authority over all the power of Satan and his wickedness. Whatever temptation may come our way God has given us the ability to endure it. We are empowered to give no place in our lives to the demonic realm. Everyday, He leads us, guides us, protects us, and provides for us. We are being taught the majesty and royalty of the ways of God to rule with the King of kings and the Lord of lords. God is our Father and we are His children so let righteousness flow out like a mighty stream.

References

Arthur G. Patzia and Anthony J. Petrotta, Pocket Dictionary of Biblical Studies (Downers Grove, IL: InterVarsity Press, 2002), 74.

BDAG – William Arndt et al., A Greek-English Lexicon of the New Testament and Other Early Christian Literature (Chicago: University of Chicago Press, 2000), 412.

Biblia Hebraica Stuttgartensia: With Werkgroep Informatica, Vrije Universiteit Morphology; Bible. O.T. Hebrew. Werkgroep Informatica, Vrije Universiteit.

Bruce, F. F. 2011. Philippians. Understanding the Bible Commentary Series.

Charles Simeon, Horae Homileticae: James to Jude, vol. 20 (London: Holdsworth and Ball, 1833), 66–67.

Charles Simeon, Horae Homileticae: Romans, vol. 15 (London: Holdsworth and Ball, 1833), 140.

Derek R. Brown, Philippians, ed. Douglas Mangum, Lexham Research Commentaries

Ronald L. Eisenberg, The JPS Guide to Jewish Traditions, 1st ed. (Philadelphia: The Jewish Publication Society, 2004), 516.

Flavius Josephus and William Whiston, The Works of Josephus: Complete and Unabridged (Peabody: Hendrickson, 1987), 484–561

Gottlob Schrenk, Theological Dictionary of the New Testament, ed. Gerhard Kittel, Geoffrey W. Bromiley, and Gerhard Friedrich (Grand Rapids, MI: Eerdmans, 1964–), 174.

Hans Wolfgang Heidland, "Λογίζομαι, Λογισμός," in Theological Dictionary of the New Testament, ed. Gerhard Kittel, Geoffrey W. Bromiley, and Gerhard Friedrich (Grand Rapids, MI: Eerdmans, 1964–), 284.

"Homilies of St. John Chrysostom, Archbishop of Constantinople, on the Epistle of St. Paul to the Romans," in Saint Chrysostom: Homilies on the Acts of the Apostles and the Epistle to the Romans, ed. Philip Schaff, trans. J. B. Morris, W. H. Simcox, and George B. Stevens, vol. 11, A Select Library of the Nicene and Post-Nicene Fathers of the Christian

Church, First Series (New York: Christian Literature Company, 1889), 403.

Johan Lust, Erik Eynikel, and Katrin Hauspie, A Greek-English Lexicon of the Septuagint : Revised Edition (Deutsche Bibelgesellschaft: Stuttgart, 2003).

Johannes P. Louw and Eugene Albert Nida, Greek-English Lexicon of the New Testament: Based on Semantic Domains (New York: United Bible Societies, 1996), 149.

John Lightfoot, A Commentary on the New Testament from the Talmud and Hebraica, Matthew-1 Corinthians, Matthew-Mark, vol. 2, 417.

Martin, Ralph P. 1974. Worship in the Early Church.

Melick, Richard R. 1991. Philippians, Colossians, Philemon. NAC. Nashville, Tenn.: Broadman & Holman Publishers.

Michael L. Rodkinson, trans., The Babylonian Talmud: Original Text, Edited, Corrected, Formulated, and Translated into English, vol. 20 (Boston, MA: The Talmud Society, 1918), 50.

Jacob Neusner, The Jerusalem Talmud: A Translation and Commentary (Peabody, Massachusetts: Hendrickson Publishers, 2008).

(Jacob Neusner, 1988) The Mishnah : A New Translation (New Haven, CT: Yale University Press, 1988), 11.

O'Brien, Peter Thomas. 1991. The Epistle to the Philippians: A Commentary on the Greek Text. NIGTC.

Osborn Grant R. , Philippians: Verse by Verse, Osborne New Testament Commentaries (Bellingham, WA: Lexham Press, 2017), 31.

Spiros Zodhiates, The Complete Word Study Dictionary: New Testament (Chattanooga, TN: AMG Publishers, 2000).

TDNT- Heinrich Schlier, "Ἀνατέλλω, Ἀνατολή," in Theological Dictionary of the New Testament, ed. Gerhard Kittel, Geoffrey W. Bromiley, and Gerhard Friedrich (Grand Rapids, MI: Eerdmans, 1964–), 351.

TDOT- Helmer Ringgren and Bo Johnson, "צָדַק," in Theological Dictionary of the Old Testament, ed. G. Johannes Botterweck and Heinz-Josef Fabry, trans. Douglas W. Stott (Grand Rapids, MI; Cambridge, U.K.: William B. Eerdmans Publishing Company, 2003), 240–241.

The Holy Bible: King James Version, 1900 Authorized Version.

The New Testament in the Original Greek: Byzantine Textform 2005, with Morphology.

Translation in the Old Tradition, 2020 Dr. Mark Spitsbergen ThD, MS

F. Weber, System d. altsynagogalen Palästinischen Theologie, p. 273 f., 1880

Werner Foerster, "Σῴζω, Σωτηρία, Σωτήρ, Σωτήριος," in Theological Dictionary of the New Testament, ed. Gerhard Kittel, Geoffrey W. Bromiley, and Gerhard Friedrich (Grand Rapids, MI: Eerdmans, 1964–), 965.)

Witherington, Ben. 2011. Paul's Letter to the Philippians: A Socio-Rhetorical Commentary.

Glossary of Scriptures

Gen. 6:9; 7:1; 12:1; 13:15; 15:4-6; 17:8; 18:23-26, 28; 19:22; 22:1-19; 26:5
Ex. 9:27; 19:6
Lev. 19:2; 26:12
Num. 23:10, 21
Deut. 6:25; 8:3; 9:4; 11:21; 18:15; 19:7; 29:4; 30:12-14; 32:4
1 Sam. 15:22
2 Chr. 20:7
Job 1:1; 19:25
Ps. 1:6; 5:12; 9:8; 10:3; 11:4-5, 7, 30; 13:25; 14:1-3; 15:1-5; 19:9; 22:3; 23:3; 24:3-6; 32:11; 34:13-17, 19; 37:25, 29; 45:6; 51:5; 53:1-3; 85:13; 89:14; 97:2, 12; 106:3; 112:6; 119:1-3, 116, 132:9; 142; 132:9; 140:13; 145:17
Prov. 2:9, 20; 8:20; 10:25; 11:5; 12:26, 28; 13:6; 15:9, 19; 16:31
Isa. 1:19; 5:16; 6:1-12; 32:17; 41:8; 51:8; 53:12; 54:17; 59:16; 60:21; 61:10; 65:17, 24
Jer. 23:5-6; 31:31-34
Ezek. 3:21; 11:19; 14:14, 20; 18:31; 26:36; 36:25-37; 47:1-12
Dan. 9:6, 24; 12:3, 9

Hos. 10:12
Am. 5:24
Hab. 2:4
Zeph. 3:5

Mt. 1:19; 3:8; 4:4; 5:3, 6, 10, 14, 16-20; 6:30, 33; 7:16; 8:10, 26; 9:2, 22, 27-29; 13:14, 17; 15:3, 6; 16:27; 17:20; 21:21; 23:23, 35; 25:37, 46

Mk. 1:11; 2:16; 7:9, 13; 10:20-21

Lk. 1:5-6, 67-75; 2:25-26; 5:30; 7:37, 39; 11:52; 12:32; 16:2, 19-31; 18:11; 20:46; 23:25, 43; 26:41

Jn. 1:12, 16-17; 3:3-6; 4:23; 5:19-20, 22, 30, 46; 6:56; 7:39; 8:12, 28-29, 56; 10:18, 27; 12:39-40, 48; 13:34; 14:10, 12-17, 20-23, 26, 31; 15:1-8; 16:13-15; 17:14, 16, 21-23; 18:12

Ac. 2:24, 33; 3:16, 22; 6:5, 8; 7:37; 10:2, 4, 45; 11:24; 14:9; 17:30-31; 20:26, 28; 26:20, 22; 28:26

Rom. 1:3-4, 8-9, 13, 17-18, 25; 2:15; 3:1-31; 4:1-25; 5:12-21; 6:1-23; 7:4-5, 12-13; 8:1-9, 11, 13-14, 29, 32; 9:1-5, 30-32; 10:1-3, 6-13, 17; 11:6; 12:1; 13:8, 10, 12, 14; 14:17; 15:16, 18

1 Cor. 1:30; 2:5; 3:13-14; 6:11, 20; 7:11; 9:7; 15:10, 17, 24, 34, 58; 16:10

2 Cor. 1:12; 3:3, 9, 13; 4:7, 11; 5:17-18, 21; 6:16; 9:8; 10:2, 4-6; 11:15; 13:5

Gal. 1:4, 6, 10, 14, 16; 2:11-13, 16-22; 3:2-3, 6, 10-11, 13, 16-17, 19, 21, 24; 4:2, 4, 6, 21-31; 5:14, 16, 18, 19-25; 6:4

Eph. 1:3, 6-7, 19, 23; 2:2-3, 6, 8-10, 12, 15-18; 3:9, 12, 17, 19-20; 4:8-9, 11, 13, 15, 20, 22-24; 5:9-11, 30; 6:2, 10

Php. 1:11, 20-21, 27; 2:12-13, 15, 30; 3:6, 9, 20

Col. 1:10-13, 27, 29; 2:9-12, 14-15; 3:1-4, 10, 20

1 Thess. 1:3; 4:1, 9; 5:13, 24

2 Thess. 1:11-12; 2:17

1 Tim. 1:9; 2:10; 5:10, 25; 6:11, 18

2 Tim. 1:10; 2:4, 6, 10, 21-22; 3:16-17

Tt. 1:16; 2:7, 12, 14; 3:1, 4-8, 14-15

Heb. 1:1-39; 2:10, 14; 3:7-19; 4:1-11; 5:8; 6:1, 10; 7:18-19, 25; 8:7-8, 10; 9:14-15; 10:1-2, 16, 19-21, 24, 38; 11:1-40; 12:2, 11, 25; 13:21

Jas. 1:13-15, 17, 21; 2:14-26

1 Pet. 1:2-3, 11-12, 14-15, 22-23; 2:1-2, 5, 12, 24-25; 3:12, 18-19

2 Pet. 1:3-10; 2:1-22; 3:13, 18

1 Jn. 1:6-7; 2:6, 27, 29; 3:4, 7-8, 10, 19, 22-24; 4:4, 12-13, 15-17; 5:11

Jude 1:3-19

Rev. 1:5; 2:7; 5:9; 7:14; 19:8

Sirach 3:14, 30; 7:10; 16:14; 29:12; 31:11; 40:17, 24
Tobit 12:8; 14:10-11

Appendix

Righteous, Righteousness, and Justice

In the Hebrew language צְדָקָה ('sedaqah') translates both righteousness and justice in the KJV. It occurs 157 times of that 15 times it is translated as "justice," 8 times as "right," 3 times as "righteous acts." The Hebrew word צְדָקָה ('sadaqah') is translated by the Greek word δικαιοσύνη ('dikaiosyne'), which makes no distinction between "righteousness" and "justice." δικαιοσύνη ('dikaiosyne') occurs 344 times in the LXX, and of that, 124 times it is translated by צְדָקָה ('sadaqah'); also צֶדֶק ('sedek').

צְדָקָה ('ṣĕdāqâ'), righteousness, righteous

n. honesty; justice; justness; community loyalty; entitlement; just cause; just deeds. Greek equiv. fr. LXX: δικαιοσύνη (122). LTW צְדָקָה (faith).

Noun Usage

1. Righteous person – a person characterized by righteous actions and morals. Related Topics: Equity; Innocence; Conscience; Justice; Integrity; Justification; Righteousness.

2. Righteousness – adherence to what is required according to a standard; for example, a moral standard, though not always. Sense Antonym: unrighteousness.

> צְדָקָה (ṣeḏā·qā(h)): n.fem.; ≡ Str 6666; TWOT 1879b —1. LN 88.12–88.23 righteousness, justice, rightness, i.e., the state of doing what is required according to a standard

James Swanson, Dictionary of Biblical Languages with Semantic Domains : Hebrew (Old Testament) (Oak Harbor: Logos Research Systems, Inc., 1997).

> 1879b   צְדָקָה ('ṣĕdāqâ') justice, righteousness.
>
> 1879c   צַדִּיק ('ṣaddîq') just, lawful, righteous.

Harold G. Stigers, "1879 צָדֵק," in Theological Wordbook of the Old Testament, ed. R. Laird Harris, Gleason L. Archer Jr., and Bruce K. Waltke (Chicago: Moody Press, 1999), 752.

The root of צְדָקָה is צדק (righteous). All of the words that are derived from צדק are listed below:

צֶדֶק ('ṣedeq'), n. accuracy, what is correct; right thing, what is honest; equity, what is right; communal loyalty; salvation, well-being. Greek equiv. fr. LXX: δικαιοσύνη (76), δίκαιος (22). LTW צֶדֶק (Justice).

Noun Usage

צֶדֶק ('ṣedeq')

1. Righteousness — adherence to what is required according to a standard; for example, a moral standard, though not always. Sense Antonym: unrighteousness.

2. Justice (quality) — the quality of being free from favoritism, self-interest, bias, or deception; especially conforming to established standards or rules. Sense Antonym: injustice (practice). Related Topic: Justice.

צְדָקָה – Righteousness or Justice
צֶדֶק – rightness, righteousness,
צִדְקִיָּהוּ – Zedekiahu
צָדוֹק – Zadok
יְהוֹצָדָק – Jehozadak

Along with four other names…

Separate root צַדִּיק (righteous, innocent, in the right) there are no other derivatives of this root. It is either translated as "righteous" or "just" by the KJV. Of the 206 times that it occurs, 145 times it refers to a righteous person. This word appears 206 times in the BHS. It is also translated by δικαιοσύνη ('dikaiosyne') in the LXX.

צַדִּיק ('ṣdyq'), Righteous

adj. just; innocent, in the right; upright, devout. Greek equiv. fr. LXX: δίκαιος (164).

Adjective Usage

1. Righteous — characterized by or proceeding from accepted standards of morality or justice. Sense Antonym: unrighteous. Related Topics: Equity; Innocence; Conscience; Justice; Integrity; Justification; Righteousness.

2. Right (morally) — in conformity with justice, law, or morality. Related Topics: Equity; Innocence; Conscience; Justice; Integrity; Justification; Righteousness.

Modern Israeli Hebrew regards צְדָקָה (ṣeḏā·qā(h) as righteousness. 'sedeq' as justice. Righteousness is a behavior and צדק ('sedeq') is regarded as that which a court should provide when someone who has been wronged.

Δικαιοσύνη, Righteous, Righteousness

δικαιοσύνη -ης, ἡ; ('dikaiosyne'), n. righteousness. Hebrew equivalent: (76) צֶדֶק, (122) צְדָקָה. LTW δικαιοσύνη (Righteousness), δικαιοσύνη (Justice).

Noun Usage

1. Righteousness – adherence to what is required according to a standard; for example, a moral standard, though not always. Sense Antonym: unrighteousness.

2. Righteousness (state) – a status of legal rectitude that satisfies the moral requirements of God's character.

The root of δικαιοσύνη is δικη (punishment meted out as legal penalty). All of those words derived from δικη that relate to biblical studies are listed below.

δικαιοσύνη, ης, ἡ ('dikaiosynē') righteousness, justice

Horst Robert Balz and Gerhard Schneider, Exegetical Dictionary of the New Testament (Grand Rapids, Mich.: Eerdmans, 1990–), 325.

δικαιοσύνη, ης, ἡ (s. δίκαιος; Theognis, Hdt.+) gener. the quality of being upright. Theognis 1, 147 defines δ. as the sum of all ἀρετή; acc. to Demosth. (20, 165) it is the opp. of κακία. A strict classification of δ. in the NT is complicated by freq. interplay of abstract and concrete aspects drawn from OT and Gr-Rom. cultures, in which a sense of equitableness combines with awareness of responsibility within a social context.

William Arndt et al., A Greek-English Lexicon of the New Testament and Other Early Christian Literature (Chicago: University of Chicago Press, 2000), 247.

Derivations of the root of δικη:

> δικαιοσύνη – Righteousness or Justice
> Δίκαιος – upright, just, fair
> Δίκαιος – demonstrate something morally right, show justice
> ἀδικέω – To do wrong, to act unjust
> Ἀδικία – wrongdoing, unrighteous deeds, wickedness, evil
> Ἄδικος – unjust, to act sinfully…
> Δικαίωμα – regulations, requirements for righteous deeds
> ἐκδίκησις – vengeance, punishment, meting out justice
> ἐκδικέω – grant justice, avenge
> Ἀδίκως – unjustly, undeserved
> δικαιοκρισία – just fair verdict, righteous judgment
> ὑπόδικος – brought to trial, guilty
> Καταδίκη – condemnation, judgement

All derivatives relate to moral conduct and behavior or to the judgment or legal consequence for those actions. The analysis of the various lemma for each of the derivatives do not reveal any significant changes in the definitions of the above words.

The word "justice" is only found in the OT 28 times and does not occur at all in the NT. It is always translated from the Hebrew words 'sedeq' and 'sedaqah.' Just is found many times in both the OT and NT. "Just" is also translated from the same words as "righteous" and "righteousness," both in the OT and NT. In the NT, it is most commonly translated from the Greek δίκαιος ('dikaios') making "just" equal to "righteous."

δίκαιος -ου, ὁ; ('dikaios'), adj. righteous; just. Hebrew equivalent: (164) צַדִּיק. LTW δίκαιος (Righteousness), δίκαιος (Justice).

Adjective Usage

1. Righteous – characterized by or proceeding from accepted standards of morality or justice. Sense Antonym: unrighteous.

2. Right (morally) – in conformity with justice, law, or morality

About the Author

Dr. Mark Spitsbergen is the Senior Pastor of the Abiding Place in San Diego, California where he and his wife Anne have pastored since 1985. He holds a Bachelor of Arts Degree (BA) in Biology/Chemistry from Point Loma Nazarene University, a Master of Science (MS) from the University of Saint Andrews, a Doctorate of Theology (ThD) from School of Bible Theology, as well as a Doctorate of Ministry (D. Min.) from Life Christian University. He has been studying Biblical languages since 1983. He began his study of biblical languages at PLNU and also studied at UCSD with Dr. David Noel Freedman.

www.ingramcontent.com/pod-product-compliance
Lightning Source LLC
LaVergne TN
LVHW011421080426
835512LV00005B/199